COACHING
TEAM
DEFENSE

Fritz Shurmur

MacGregor Sports Education
Waukesha, Wisconsin

Library of Congress Cataloging-in-Publication Data

Shurmur, Fritz.
    Coaching team defense.

    1. Football — Defense.   2. Football — Coaching.
I. Title
GV951.18.S48   1989   796.332'07'7   88-31387
ISBN 0-941175-26-X

ISBN 0-941175-26-X

Dedication

To Peggy Jane, whose patience, understanding, and support through all the good and especially the not-so-good times make her an incredibly special coach's wife and mother. To our kids — Sally Ann the writer, Scott the doctor, and Susie the teacher — who have been and always will be great sources of pride to us.

To the many coaches and players I have been privileged to work with over the past thirty-five years. They are the reasons going to work every day has been so enjoyable.

About The Author

For many years, Fritz Shurmur has been regarded as one of the top defensive coaches in the country. The defensive units he has been associated with, at both the collegiate and professional levels, have been characterized by their tenaciousness, as well as by their physical and intelligent play. The defensive units Shurmur has coached have been characterized as intense, the major characteristic used to describe the coach, both on and off the field.

A 1954 graduate of Albion (Michigan) College, Shurmur earned four varsity letters in both football and baseball. He captained the 1953 football squad, earning all-league honors at center, and was named the most valuable player of both his team and league. He also won all-conference recognition as a second baseman on the 1954 baseball team. His achievements were not limited to the athletic field as he was elected to Omicron Delta Kappa, men's honorary society, president of Alpha Tau Omega social fraternity, and president of the senior class.

A physical education major as an undergraduate, he earned a master's degree in educational administration from Albion in 1956.

Shurmur joined the Albion staff after graduation and coached swimming and football there for eight years. In 1961, Albion's Britons won their third MIAA league title in four years, compiling an 8-0 record as Shurmur's defensive unit won league honors, yielding only 556 yards rushing.

Shurmur moved to the University of Wyoming in 1962 as defensive line coach. Under his tutelage, the Pokes became the only major college football team to win as many as two defensive titles during the 1960s: rushing and total defense. In 1966 and 1967, the Cowboys were the best in rushing defense, and in 1968 they topped the list in total defense.

Shurmur's tough and disciplined unit also paced the Western Athletic Conference in defense in 1963, 1965, 1966, and 1967. Shurmur's defensive unit led the Pokes to a Sun Bowl victory in 1966 and to the Sugar Bowl just one year later.

After serving as head coach at Wyoming from 1971 through the 1974 season, he moved to the Detroit Lions of the National Football League as defensive line coach. He was named defensive coordinator in 1977 and served in that capacity through that season.

In 1978 Shurmur moved to New England as the Patriots' defensive line coach. He coached with the Patriots for four years and was the team's defensive coordinator the last two. In 1979, his defensive line led the NFL with 57 quarterback sacks. The 1978 Patriots team compiled an 11-5 record and won the AFC East division title.

In 1982 Shurmur was named defensive line coach by the Los Angeles Rams, serving in that capacity one year. In 1983, when John Robinson was appointed head coach, he named Shurmur the defensive coordinator and inside linebacker coach. Shurmur's first year in that capacity saw the defense improve dramatically, moving up 12 places in the league rankings. Each year since, the defense has made significant progress to the point where the Rams are now regarded as one of the best defensive teams in the NFL. This rise to national prominence by the defense has been a huge factor in contributing to four successive playoff years for the Rams.

Shurmur is a firm believer in the potential for greatness that is possible when people work hard together. His philosophy of coaching is built on a strong commitment to the team, its goals, and objectives. It is his belief that, without exception, the most successful teams have been those that have had a strong emphasis on "the team."

This book is about the important factors in keeping the other team out of the end zone. It is about coaching defense with the basic idea of getting as many as possible of the eleven players on the field to the ball. It is written for the football coach at any level of play and regardless of coaching experience or philosophy. Coach Shurmur's primary motivation in writing this book was to make available to coaches the type of information about defense that he wished was available during his early coaching career.

Contents

1

Goals
And
Objectives

PREVENT THE SCORE

There is no question that the number one objective of a defensive football team is to keep the opponent from scoring. I know this point would seem to be so obvious that it need not be mentioned. However, in the past few years there has been such a widespread emphasis on statistics, it appears at times that the number of yards gained rushing or passing, or the opponent's first downs, sacks, or interceptions, are more important than the number of points scored on a defense.

The total defensive unit — players and coaches — has to believe in this as the number one goal of the defensive team. All it takes is one position coach who is trying to gain some notoriety for himself and his players to get in the way of a total defensive team accepting this as their number one goal.

A defensive line coach obsessed with the number of sacks, a linebacker coach overly concerned with the number of tackles, or a secondary coach who sees only the number of interceptions as the major concern are all examples of ways that the men responsible for reinforcing the major objective of a defensive team may, by intent or accident, create obstacles to the success of the group. Whenever this occurs, it is the responsibility of the coordinator or whoever is in charge to redirect or refocus the individual or group that is involved.

PREVENT THE BIG PLAY

Nothing has a bigger negative impact on a defensive team than when an opponent makes a long run or completes a long pass. Big plays against a defense usually occur when there is some kind of a breakdown by the defensive team. Preventing the big play in the running game involves getting great pursuit to the football followed by good tackling when the defense gets there. In the passing game it involves effective pass rush with coverage that does not allow the pass to be completed beyond the deep defenders.

Each defensive player must be constantly reminded of the importance of breaking or running to the ball when it is thrown. It is very important that defensive teams practice running to the ball or pursuing and breaking on the ball when it is thrown. Each coach has the responsibility to demand that his players run to the ball on every play in practice.

The defensive scheme employed by a team can be very important in determining the type of exposure a team has to "big plays".

For example, dogging, blitzing, man-for-man football teams are, by design, used to pressure offensive teams into errors or big plays. But, by adopting these approaches, the chances of the offense making a big play on the defense also increase. These schemes emphasize individual matchups, big play capacity, and pressuring the opponent's offense into mistakes. Increased opportunities for big plays by the defense are always accompanied by the high risk of greater opportunities for big plays by the opponent's offense.

I am convinced teams that employ a reading defensive scheme with a minimum of dogs and blitzes and play mostly zone coverage are not as susceptible to the big offensive play. It is true that this more conservative approach does not create as many opportunities for big plays by the defense. But this type of philosophy *does* decrease the exposure to big plays by the offense. And there is no question that reading defensive teams put more players in a position to pursue the ball than do penetrating and blitzing defenses. The utilization of zone coverages makes it more difficult to get the big play in the passing game by getting behind the secondary.

Patience and a commitment to play the percentages are important factors in a team's ability to play with a focus on preventing the big play. If a defensive team adopts a scheme that is conservative or containing in approach, it cannot become upset with temporary successes by the offensive team. A few successful passes, running plays, or first downs cannot become issues to the point of causing the defense to lose confidence, panic, and depart from its basic philosophy.

A team that adopts the containing philosophy must play the percentages all the way. For example, it makes very little sense for a team to play zone and basic schemes all over the field and then, just because the offense gets the ball in a short yardage situation or inside the twenty-five-yard line, switch to a dogging, blitzing defense, increasing the exposure to a big play or a scoring play.

THREE AND OUT

It is the responsibility of the defense to put their offense back on the field in as good a field position as possible. This is best accomplished, of course, by limiting the opponent's ability to make first downs. The basic approach here is to go on the field as a defensive team to play three downs, force the opponent to punt, and put the offense back on the field in a good position. Each defensive player must understand that the ideal way to attack the offense is to dictate to the opponent, as quickly as possible in a series of downs, what the opponent must do to maintain possession — that is, put them in long yardage as quickly as possible.

The goal on first down has to be to hold the opponent's gain to less than three yards. If a defensive team does this, it has dictated to the offense what it must do to maintain possession. The defense has limited the opponent's offense, increased the predictability factor, and increased the opportunities for the defense to make a big play.

There are a lot of great defensive calls that can be made on second and long — very few on second down and five yards or less.

TURNOVERS — INTERCEPTIONS AND FUMBLES

I know many coaches claim to "coach turnovers" on defense, and I marvel at their resourcefulness. I do notice, however, that many of the teams that are very high in this area one year are at the other end of the spectrum the next under the same coaching staff. I do think it is difficult to come up with concrete definitive ways to create fumbles and interceptions. I do not think it is difficult to coach ways to put players in a better position to be more opportunistic in these areas.

For example, logic tells us that the greater number of our players who are around the ball, the better our chances of recovering a fumble should one occur, either by chance or our efforts in tackling. Our emphasis on pursuit and breaking on the ball, along with hard tackling, are all factors that increase our chances to force and recover fumbles.

Pass interceptions usually occur more frequently with zone coverage teams. This is true largely because the pass defenders are placed in a position facing the quarterback with no man-for-man responsibility, whereas a player in man-for-man coverage has his back to the quarterback much of the time, chasing the man he is covering.

It is very important that the ball be made the issue in coaching zone coverage. Reading patterns, breaking on the ball, and catching the ball are all very important coaching points. The pass rush hurrying the quarterback, with the rushers' hands up forcing a high trajectory of the ball or obstructing the quarterback's vision, are all important factors in creating more opportunities for interceptions.

SCORING ON DEFENSE

Scoring on defense usually occurs more with teams whose basic scheme is pressure, dogging, and blitzing. These teams score by forcing the offense into a huge error and capitalizing on it. Although reading zone teams are not as apt to score on defense forcing the big error by pressure, they have the capacity for defensive touchdowns.

Scoring opportunities are created by the team factor of coordinated effort, pursuit, and breaking on the thrown ball. I have always felt that the defensive coordinator has the responsibility to continually emphasize the goals and objectives of a defensive team. Each member of the group — coach and player — must be reminded on a regular basis of the critical factors that determine the success of a defensive team.

2

Personnel: Physical Qualifications

MOVEMENT

The ability to run is very high on the list of qualities needed for effective defensive players. Speed is at the very foundation of a team's defensive scheme if its major objective is to get as many as possible of its eleven defensive men to the ball on every play. Team speed is the one factor that determines how well a team pursues the run, rushes the passer or plays pass coverage.

Not far behind speed in importance is the ability to change directions. Although there are many definitions of this skill, I think it is best described as the player's ability to take the quickest, shortest course to the ball in an opposite direction. The ability to change directions quickly — from going right to going left and vice versa as well as moving from front to back and back to front quickly — is the movement skill all good defensive players possess. The ability to break flat and take direct routes is also crucial.

In order to change directions effectively, the player must be able to play with his body weight distributed over the balls of his feet. This type of weight distribution requires that the upper body (that is, above the waist) be positioned so that the shoulders are approximately over the feet. Good defensive players must also be able to play with good flexion at the ankle and hips and be "knee benders." Players who do not display this kind of flexibility are usually limited

5

in their ability to "make plays" on defense. This ability to change direction has a lot to do with the physical makeup and sometimes the body type of the athlete. I do think that this skill can be developed and improved upon with coaching. Off-season conditioning programs, warm-up routines, and individual breakdown drill periods are ideal times to work on improving these qualities.

QUICKNESS OR AGILITY

I describe quickness or agility as the ability to avoid obstacles by moving or picking up the feet quickly and under control. Again, the ability to play with his feet under him is a critical prerequisite for "the agile player". The player who plays defense effectively must be able to move his feet quickly to avoid blockers, to adjust angles to the ball carrier or passer, or to move around and over the debris that inevitably collects on the defensive side of the scrimmage line after the snap. Developing and improving this skill is important since the defensive side of the line of scrimmage is more like an obstacle course than an open highway.

And, similar to qualities described in preceding paragraphs, while "innate ability" in this area is important, it is also a skill that can be improved upon with practice and coaching. Any drills that require the player to work his feet rapidly, change speeds and directions under control, or react while he is working his feet over obstacles such as dummies are all activities that can contribute to improving the skill.

STRENGTH OR LEVERAGE

There was a time in the evolution of the game of football when strength was the most crucial physical requirement to play defense. This dates back to when football was, by offensive design, played in a more conservative fashion. It was before the advent of the wide-open pro passing offenses, the veer option, or the wishbone. These offensive concepts, along with their many variations, forced defenses to defend "all of the field" all of the time, placing a higher priority on running and movement in all defensive players.

Strength is definitely an asset to defensive players but it is extremely important that strength development not come at the expense of speed and the ability to move. Monitoring and continued evaluation of a player's quickness and speed is essential during those periods in an athlete's development when he is lifting weights and acquiring bulk to increase his strength.

There are some athletes who are "naturally strong". These players seem to develop a high degree of strength through the natural maturation process with little conscious effort on their part. However, most of what we observe in the way of strength in defensive football players today is developed. Weight-training programs at all levels have produced exceedingly strong, bulked-up football players.

Possessing great strength does not ensure an athlete's success as a defensive football player. The ability to utilize strength as a tool to play the game better is really the key here. There are many weight lifters who have great strength but lack the ability to use it playing football. The type of strength we are looking for in defensive players is the type that allows them to defeat blockers, win the one-on-one battles, and change the direction of the ball carrier when they tackle him. This kind of power is usually described as "explosive strength." It is probably best described as a player's ability to play the game using all his strength or power, under control, without having to slow down to use it.

Another aspect of strength as it applies to football is leverage, or the ability to utilize the big muscle groups. In a general way we are referring to the muscle groups below the waist. Generally the player who is in the best leverage position wins the one-on-one contests that occur in football. The ability to play with leverage is determined by those same body position factors we referred to in the movement areas; flexion at the ankles and hips, the player's ability to bend at the knees — all are crucial in utilizing the big muscles. A good point of reference is the position of the head and eyes of the defensive player. As he focuses on the offensive opponent, his head and eyes should be lower than those of the offensive man he is trying to defeat. If the defensive player assumes this position and has the proper flexion in the critical areas, he should be in a better position to use his strength and defeat the offensive player.

All the preceding points are important in the utilization of strength, whether we are talking about striking a blow with the forearm, using a hand shiver, tackling, or utilizing any other of the many techniques employed by defensive players.

Obviously the strength factor is a bigger requisite for linemen or linebackers than it would be for defensive backs. Strength and power are great assets for defensive football players and much of the time go a long way in determining the level of success. It is again important to point out that strength must be accompanied by leverage and cannot be developed at the expense of or used as a substitute for movement.

HOW THESE PHYSICAL QUALITIES
IMPROVE THE DEFENSIVE PLAYER

The bottom line here is how these physical qualities apply to making the defensive player a better performer.

Obviously these traits exist in varying degrees in all athletes. Those who are faster, bigger, stronger, and quicker usually are the best players, provided the proper temperament and motivational factors are present.

Although most of these physical qualities are innate or part of the individual makeup, they can all be developed or improved with coaching and dedicated effort on the part of the athlete. It is the coach's responsibility to develop programs, drills, and practice routines that will increase the player's athletic ability.

The ability to "make plays" on defense, to defeat or avoid blockers, knock down or intercept passes, and make tackles is increased in proportion to the development of these physical skills. The higher the level of individual development in these areas, the more effective and productive will be the efforts of the defensive team in preventing "the score."

3

Personnel: Mental Qualifications

PLAY HARD

The ability to play hard all the time is something all coaches aspire to get out of their teams. I am really convinced that defensive teams whose members are able to do this compete at a very high level most of the time. I don't think this level of play just happens — it must be developed by coaches and coaching staffs who have a real belief in the importance of this characteristic. What we are talking about here is the ability of each member of the defensive unit to work at competing as close as possible to his optimum level on every defensive play. It is the responsibility of each coach to demand that the players he coaches practice and play games at this level. Coaches and players can never accept anything other than maximum effort on every play.

Despite this, however, teams often don't play up to their maximum effort, and there are a number of reasons for this. Sometimes coaches get so caught up in the technical aspects of the game that they lose sight of the importance of continually reinforcing the place of intensity and effort in playing defense. Another reason teams don't play hard all the time is that coaches tend to make the game too complex. They ask their players to remember so many different defenses, alignments, stunts, blitzes, or coverages that they spend their time thinking — not reacting. Players who are forced to think too much are limited in their ability to play the game with great velocity. I am convinced that a simple defensive system that lends itself to repetition and does not require complex adjustment is best.

It is the responsibility of the coaching staff to develop this type of scheme. Players who are sure of the reactions desired in the various situations because they have experienced them over and over again will play defense with great velocity because they are not slowed down by the thought process. All players have the ability to play hard all the time. It is up to the coaching staff to create the type of environment that will allow a player to compete in this manner.

PLAY EFFICIENTLY

Playing hard but inefficiently equals wasted effort. Defensive teams that play efficiently are made up of players who do not make mental errors. In short, they do not help their opponent advance the ball by missing assignments or incurring penalties. These types of errors are the result of a lack of concentration on the player's part. Again, the coach's responsibility is to be certain he is not asking the players to do so many and varied responses and techniques that it is impossible to play with a high degree of efficiency. It is the player's responsibility to concentrate in meetings, film sessions, practice, and games in order to avoid making these types of errors. A well-prepared player who has concentrated, studied, and learned will perform with a high degree of efficiency. By the same token, players who think about other things, who are not focused in every learning and playing situation, are compromising their margins and are increasing their chances of making mental errors.

Playing efficiently requires that the defensive coaches continually point out to the players the essential elements needed to avoid helping the opponent. Defensive team and individual meetings, film sessions, and practices are the occasions where this type of reinforcement takes place. The actual execution by the player takes place in practice and games. Again it is the coach's responsibility to create an environment in practice that is as much like a game situation as possible. For example, field position, down and distance, and specific game situations such as short yardage, goal line, inside the twenty-five-yard line and two-minute are all important contributing factors determining specific responses required by players in games. It is critical that all these elements be included in practice situations over and over again. This type of specific preparation in practice is essential to raising the efficiency level of a defensive team in games.

PLAY TOGETHER

There is probably no skill more important in coaching a defensive team to a high level of achievement than the ability to get a team to play together. The skilled defensive coach is able to instill in his players a commitment to the team and its goals. This involves players' assuming roles as members of the group first, placing individual goals in a secondary position. Team and individual goals do not have to conflict but their order of importance is without question in a team sport.

Defensive teams with the ability to play well together are made up of individuals who are able to talk in terms of *we* or *us*, not *I* or *me*. The players in this type of unit are able to suppress their own egos for the good of the group. They are convinced that teams that play well together are made up of unselfish individuals who put team goals, achievements, and recognition ahead of their own.

This type of attitude in a defensive unit is developed, it doesn't just happen. It must be developed and reinforced by the coordinator or whoever is in charge. It all starts with the coaches themselves continually talking in terms of the team — *we* and *us*. It cannot develop if each coach talks in terms of his defense or his secondary or his linebackers. The head coach is the man ultimately held responsible for the success of "the team." He is therefore the one person on the coaching staff who can talk in terms of "his" offense, defense, or special teams. In recent years it has become popular to single out defensive coordinators as autonomous captains of their own ships. The better policy would be to avoid setting a coach apart from the group in this way, or at least keep it to a minimum.

It is especially important that the person in charge of the defense be a "team player" if the unit he is responsible for is going to have any chance of performing at a high level "as a team."

DEVELOPING COACHING STANDARDS

It is very difficult to execute any athletic skill or technique perfectly all the time. This is especially true in football where so many variables are involved in each play. That is why it is so difficult to find, even in the best of teams, a play where all eleven players are doing exactly the right thing. The critical point here, however, is that although perfection in execution is difficult to achieve, it must be the goal of every player on every play.

It is the coach's responsibility to develop a scheme that requires a base of well-defined techniques in order to execute it well. The ability to establish high standards for the execution of these skills, along with the creation of an environment for the development of them, is as crucial as any ability a coach must possess.

The coach must create practice situations where the development and improvement of these techniques can take place. The players' progress must be monitored by the coaches on a continual basis. The really good coaches are those who are coaching, emphasizing, and reinforcing the same points, with the same emphasis, during the last practice or game of the season as they were in early fall camp.

I have always believed that we as humans are geared to operate at minimums, not optimums. Most of us think we are going all out or doing something as well as we can when, most of the time, we are operating at a level far short of our maximum in the area of performance.

Coaches have the responsibility to encourage players to work toward *optimum* levels of performance and execution, in the belief that, as individuals, we get from ourselves only what we demand in the way of performance. If our standards are low, we achieve at a low level. If, on the other hand, our expectations are high and we strive for perfection in execution, our chances for achieving high levels of success are greater.

For that reason, coaches must demand a high level of execution from their players at all times. It is easy to get so caught up in the broader aspects of the game that we lose sight of those "little things" that are very often the difference between winning and losing.

4

Defending
The
Run

PRESSURE

The most important factor in defending the run is the ability of the defense to pressure or come after the offense. I don't believe there can be any lateral or flat pursuit thinking in the defensive scheme if it is to be effective in stopping the run. When defensive players are coached to play the game only on a lateral or parallel-to-the-line-of scrimmage basis, two things usually happen, and they are both bad. One is that parallel or lateral usually means the defenders' getting knocked back by the momentum of the offensive blocker. This happens if the defensive man is more concerned with pursuing parallel than pressuring through the blockers forward or attacking the offense. The other is that this type of lateral pursuit leads to defensive players' ending up in a head-up position on ball carriers. This is a poor position from which to make a tackle because it gives the offensive player the option to make a cut on the defender who is usually at some sort of an athletic ability disadvantage.

GAME OF ANGLES

The defense has to be designed to pressure the offense in order to squeeze or compress it. This is best accomplished by having the defense reduce the angles by attacking the offense on their side of the line of scrimmage. For example, in forcing the run at the perimeter it is essential that the player responsible for forcing or keeping the football inside does his job by defeating blockers on the offensive side of the line of scrimmage as close to a forty-five-degree angle as possible. This forces the ball carrier to make a decision to turn up inside quicker than he wants to and also squeezes or compresses the lane available to him to run the ball.

Another example of pressure-reducing angles is the defensive end away from a running play. He is usually responsible for the backside guard-tackle gap on plays run to the other side of center. If he is taught to catch and read as opposed to attacking the offensive blocker, he is either knocked back or at best cut off on the defensive side of the line of scrimmage. When this happens, the ball carrier will have at his disposal a huge bubble or cutback lane. However, if the defensive end is coached to attack the line of scrimmage and close the guard-tackle gap aggressively up the field, he will be pressuring, reducing, or squeezing the cutback area.

ALIGNMENTS

The most difficult position from which to play defense is head up or nose up on an offensive player. This defensive alignment is advantageous to the offensive player because it gives him a two-way go or the option to either block or cut right or left or to the inside or outside of a defender. There are times, however, when this alignment is advantageous to the defensive player. This is usually when an alignment or scheme requires the defender to be responsible for two gaps or holes on the line of scrimmage — that is, the area on either side of the offensive man opposite the defender.

I happen to think that although it is more difficult to execute most techniques from this position, the head-up or two-gap alignment is the best to use with the defensive lineman in the thirty-four or three-man-line defenses. This alignment provides a great opportunity for the ends and nose tackle to unload, attack, or pressure the offensive linemen and drive them in a backward direction. This theory of creating a new line of scrimmage by attacking with a two-gap technique is at the very core of stopping the run in the thirty-four defense. It also allows the linemen to protect the inside linebackers by making it more difficult for the offensive tackles and the center to have a clean or uninhibited release. It is crucial that, if this type of alignment technique is used with the defensive line, the linebackers are coached to compensate or to make the proper adjustments.

The advantage to a defensive player in lining up either inside or outside an offensive man is that by his alignment, the defender has taken away an option from the offensive player. For example, a defender who lines up on the outside of a blocker makes it more difficult for the offensive man to hook or to reach block him on outside plays. When a defensive player gains something by alignment, he usually gives up something else. By using an outside alignment the defensive man is in a better or stronger position against any type of outside play to his side but has become more vulnerable to being blocked out on inside plays or cut-off blocked on plays run to the other side of the center. The key here is that the defender knows the areas in which his alignment has made him more vulnerable and adjusts his play accordingly.

The same general principles apply to all defensive players with respect to alignment. It is especially important that defensive backs avoid the head-up position on potential receivers, whether they are playing zone or man-for-man coverages. The general rule is that the more space the receiver has to operate in, the more critical it is that the defensive player remove all possibility of two-way cuts or option routes by the receiver.

POSITIVE GAP CONTROL

The areas between the offensive linemen are called gaps. Offensive teams usually call them holes and give each one a number. Defensive teams normally designate each gap with a letter. In most cases the gap between the center and guard is the "A" gap, the one between the guard and tackle the "B" gap, between the tackle and tight end the "C" gap, and the area outside the tight end the "D" gap. Positive gap control means that on every running play there is a defender responsible for each gap.

The responsibility for each of these gaps is assigned to a player, usually depending on whether the ball is run to his side of the center or the opposite side. It is very important that in developing a defensive scheme the coaches give specific gap assignments to each position on all running plays. This approach leaves little room for confusion or doubt on the part of the player. It also allows the coach to fix responsibility for making defensive plays and takes all the guess work out of knowing who did or did not execute his assignment on a specific play.

It is also important that defensive players are coached to understand that the gaps move and therefore their gap responsibility moves as the running play develops. As the ball moves laterally after the snap and the blocking scheme involves the defensive players, they must react by executing their gap assignment as the play is developing. It is essential to point out here the importance of the defensive men attacking or pressuring the offense toward the offensive side of the line of scrimmage as they execute their gap control. This type of upfield pressure, as has been described earlier, reduces the angles and options for the offense and makes the gaps smaller. If players' pursuit lanes to the ball are only lateral and not toward the offense, the chances for the opening up of wide cutback lanes are greater.

COORDINATING THE RUN FORCE

Every defensive scheme has a specific defender assigned to forcing the run or making the ball carrier cut back. It is usually a secondary man, outside linebacker, or, in some alignments, it may even be a lineman.

There are four basic elements to forcing the outside run in zone coverages. They are force, fill or cutback, support or run pass, and contain. Each of these elements has a specific player or players responsible for its execution on every running play.

The force man is the defender who is responsible for tackling or making sure the ball carrier does not get outside him. It is his responsibility either to tackle the ball carrier or to force him to cut back into the pursuit pattern. Defensive backs are most often used in that role but outside linebackers as well as defensive ends are also used in some defensive schemes as run force men.

Of the deep defenders, the strong safety is usually in the best position to force because his alignment in the area of the tight end gives him the best look at those perimeter blocks that require his quick reaction to turn the play inside. The strong safety's physical stature usually lends itself more readily to the physical stress involved in taking on blockers and tackling. Cornerbacks are used as force men more by adjustment to specific formation than by defensive design. However, whenever two deep zone defenses or strong or weak zones with corner force are used, they are asked to assume this role. The outside linebackers are very often used as force men. This usually happens with man-for-man schemes, dogs, or blitzes or in change-ups in zone coverages. Defensive ends become run forcers when they are the widest defenders on the line of scrimmage. This happens most in four-man-line defenses on the open side or the side away from the tight end.

The fill or cutback man is the defensive player responsible for tackling the ball carrier after the force man has caused him to turn back inside. When a safety or corner is designated as the force man, the fill or cutback responsibility usually belongs to the outside linebacker. If the force is being executed by the outside linebacker in zone coverage, a defensive back is usually designated as the cutback man. In man-for-man coverages, dogs, or blitzes, the inside linebackers or the pursuit pattern in general has to take care of the cutback lane.

The support man is the defensive back to the side of the play who is assigned to serve as a backup to the force man and cover the deep receiver on the halfback run pass option play. In a three-deep zone defense with safety force, it is the corner and when corner force is used, it is the safety.

In a two-deep defense the safety to the side of the play is the support man. In man-for-man coverages a support man is possible only in defenses with a free safety or when a deep defender's base man-for-man responsibility blocks, thus freeing him to become a support man or deep pass defender on the halfback run-pass option play.

The contain man is the player responsible for any reverse or wide cutbacks. He is the player who, by either alignment or stunt, ends up as the widest defender on the line of scrimmage away from the initial direction of the offensive play. Usually an outside linebacker or defensive end has this assignment but stunts can place an inside linebacker or defensive tackle in this position.

Much like positive gap control with the inside run, assigning specific responsibilities on outside runs eliminates any chance of ambiguity or doubt on the part of the player. It allows coaches to be specific in the responses demanded from each player in the various alignments employed.

PURSUIT

Defensive schemes are designed to get as many of the eleven defensive players as possible to the ball carrier on every play. It is possible to judge the overall level of intensity of a defensive team by how well they run to the ball. This is a good criterion for gauging not only the fervor with which a team plays but also the skill with which it executes technique. The abilities to defeat blockers, accelerate off blocks, and avoid blockers along with the overall speed of the players are all apparent by the effectiveness with which a team pursues.

The elements of pressure and up-and-in angles are critical to the development of good pursuit. The only player in the pursuit pattern who should have an outside-in angle on the ball carrier is the force man. He should be taught to force up the field squeezing the cutback lane as he pressures the ball carrier inside. In order to compress the cutback lane, his angle should be as close to an outside-in angle of forty-five degrees as possible. He is the man in the defense who should be tackling and taking on blockers with his inside arm and shoulder. The support man or other defenders will play from the outside in only when they replace the force man should he lose outside leverage on the football or get blocked.

All other defenders except the contain man are inside-out pursuers. That is, they will maintain inside position on the football as they pursue. They must proceed laterally, gaining as much ground as possible toward the offense as they move to the ball. Again, the up-and-in theory of reducing cutback angles is crucial to good team pursuit. I have always thought that a good gauge of distance and lateral relationship with the ball carrier is for the defender to keep the ball an arm's length or about a yard in front of him. The logic here is that maintaining this position allows the defender to take the cutback away by his inside position. This location relative to the ball carrier also prevents the defender from getting head up with the man with the ball, which would put the defender at a tremendous disadvantage because it gives the ball carrier a two-way go.

Overpursuit or overrunning the ball carrier can be a bigger problem for inside pursuers than not getting there in time. That is another reason why defenders pursuing inside out must be coached to pursue up and in or toward the offense, establishing their inside-out angles as they go. Players must be reminded over and over again that when the ball is moving laterally, the ball carrier is usually three or four yards from the line of scrimmage. When he turns up the field, the defender has ample time to close inside out and make the tackle for a loss or no gain. It is when the tackler gets head up with the offensive man or overruns him that the loss of the angle advantage by the defense turns into big gains for the offense.

USING THE HANDS

There is no skill or technique more important to the defensive player than the ability to use his hands. This technique is critical for all players at all positions if they are to play their positions effectively. A defensive lineman using his hands to defeat a blocker, gain operating space, and pursue the ball carrier — a linebacker using his hands to ward off a blocker and make the tackle — a defensive back playing off an offensive man to force the football — these are just a few examples of how important the use of this technique is to playing football on the defensive side of the ball.

Football rules allow the use of the hands to ward off, avoid, or defeat blockers. This is an advantage the defense has over the offense. I think the ability of the defensive coaches to teach this technique determines, to a large part, how well a defensive team plays.

Generally there are three basic categories of techniques employed with the hands. One is the power, two-gap, or leverage technique that is used most often by the defensive line and linebackers. In this technique the strength of the blow comes from the quickness with which the blow is struck and the extension or locking of the arms and the involvement of the big muscles. It is essential that there be no hitching or winding up and that all movement of the hands and arms be forward. The blow is struck with the palms and heels of the hands, with ideal hand placement being under the shoulder pads of the offensive man at approximately the outside tips of the player's numbers. The extension of the arms or locking out at the elbows along with the rolling of the hips under the defensive man finishes the power aspect of this technique. In order not to raise up or to maintain a power-position advantage over the blocker from start to finish in the execution of this technique, it is crucial that the shoulder level of the defensive player stay down. I think this can best be accomplished if the defender always keeps his head and eyes up but focused, with his face mask lower than that of the offensive man.

The second of the hand techniques is the one used against blockers who are trying to cut, scramble, or chop-block. At times it may be necessary to give or lose a little ground in the execution of these techniques. The offensive man is trying to get under a defensive player's "block protection" when he executes these types of low blocks. In order not to let the blocker get to his legs, the defender has to be able to extend the arms and bend at the ankles, knees and hips. Again, it is important that all the movement of the hands and arms be forward and that there be no false movement. Exactly where the blow will be struck on the offensive man depends on the elevation at which he is trying to block. This will vary all the way from under the player's pads, if he is blocking relatively high, to the tips of the shoulders if he is scramble blocking. It is important that the defensive player have good flexion at the ankles, knees, and hips so that he can have some force behind the blow he is striking with the hands. The more he bends the more power he will have behind his blow. It is a critical coaching point to have players overemphasize the bending aspect — the lower the better. If they do not bend when trying to defeat blockers who are blocking them low, the blockers break through the hands and get to the defender's legs.

The third technique is the slip, slide, or drop step. These techniques involve the defensive player using his hands to avoid or finesse blockers. They involve the defensive men using their hands to simulate striking a blow, then slipping or avoiding the blocker to make the tackle. Basically a slip technique involves the defensive man avoiding a blocker by driving his hands at the offensive man like he does in a power move, then either giving ground to get by the blocker or using his movements to pull the blocker by and sliding underneath him to make the tackle. The drop step is used against a drive blocker by driving the hands at the offensive man then just before contact is made, dropping a hand, pulling a leg back, and using the momentum of the blocker to avoid contact to get to the ball carrier.

The use of the hands gives players techniques to use to defeat or avoid blockers in the running game. But, just as important is that the proper use of the hands enables defensive players to achieve "operating space." This is the separation that comes from the extension of the hands and arms that allows the defenders to get away from blockers and pursue the ball carrier.

TACKLING

All good defensive teams tackle well. Size, speed, strength, agility, and all those other traits make very little difference if a team can't tackle. Every player at every position has to be able to tackle well if a defense is going to be successful. Tackling is a skill that can be taught and improved, much like any other skill in football. I know that a lot of coaches at all levels feel that intensity and desire are about ninety percent responsible for good tackling. These same coaches allow about ten percent for technique. I think desire is certainly important, but coaches must place a much higher premium on the development of technique as an important factor in good tackling.

Tackling and methods of teaching this technique have probably changed more over the years than any of the other skills associated with the game. Much of this change has come about as a result of advances by coaches in the development of techniques. However, this is the one area where public scrutiny and the concern for safety has brought changes. The contribution of the medical profession in this area has been important in establishing guidelines.

I have always had some basic rules I tried to follow in teaching tackling. I never like to teach tackling full go or live. I think it is always better to walk through, gradually picking up the tempo but never do tackling drills more than half speed. The other is that I always try to get the ball carrier and tacklers as close together as the particular drill will allow. This, of course, minimizes the collision by reducing the distance players have in which to gain momentum before impact. I do not think it wise to turn technique teaching periods into toughness drills.

Body position is as critical to good tackling as it is to the execution of any technique in football. A good base, weight distributed over the balls of the feet along with good flexion at the ankles, knees, and hips are all very important.

The ability to react quickly, adjust to changes in directions, and the ability to change the direction of the ball carrier are all dependent upon the defensive player's ability to play defense in a "good football position."

After many years of teaching tackling, I think that aside from the importance of body position, there are only two critical coaching points. One is focus or the ability to keep the head and eyes up or focused on the target. The other is the ability to use the hands and arms to grab the ball carrier and get him to the ground.

The ability to see the target and adjust to changes of direction is very important. I feel that in order to tackle effectively the defensive man has to have his eyes focused on the target — the numbers of the offensive man. His head and eyes have to be up and focused from start to finish of the technique. He has to be able to see any change in the elevation of the ball carrier as well as any change of direction. The key here is that the tackler must keep his power base by keeping his shoulder level lower than the ball carrier's while he keeps his head and eyes focused on the tips of the ball carrier's numbers. As the ball carrier gets lower, so must the tackler adjust by flexing or bending more at the ankle, knees, and hips. I believe more tackles are missed because players took their eyes off the target than for any other reason.

I coached for many years before it became apparent to me that one of the most important parts of the tackling technique was the tackler's ability to grab and hang onto the ball carrier. In my earlier years of coaching we taught tacklers to use the hands by grasping one with the other to lock up around the ball carrier's waist or the lower portion of the rib cage. The other use of the hands we taught was to wrap the hands and arms around the legs on low tackles.

I firmly believe that along with body position and focusing on the target, the use of the hands to grab the ball carrier and hang on is a huge factor in good tackling. The technique is executed by the driving of the hands toward the upper outside tips of the numbers on the front of the ball carrier's jersey. The blow is struck with the palm and heels of the hands and as the hands make contact, the tackler grabs the jersey with both hands. Even though the teaching of this skill is done at a walking pace initially, it is important that the tackler drive the hands, grab the jersey, extend or lock out at the elbows, and actually change the direction of the ball carrier by knocking him back. It is important that the defender attack the ball carrier forward and make contact on the offensive side of the imaginary line of scrimmage. This again is consistent with the up-and-in theory of attacking the offense.

In practicing this technique, it is very important that the defensive men who are acting as ball carriers make quick lateral moves as they approach the defender to force him to focus on the target and adjust to movement. All the cuts by the ball carrier should be flat or parallel to force the defender to adjust laterally in larger areas. These lateral cuts are important too, because we want to minimize the force of the collision. We do not want the teaching of this technique to become the development or evaluation of toughness.

It is also important that whenever the ball carrier makes a cut and begins to go by the tackler that the defensive man throws his hand and arm across the body to the far number, grabs the jersey, and hangs on.

The ball carriers are never taken to the ground in the teaching of this technique. The actual drills always finish with the tackler grasping the jersey of the ball carrier, elbows locked with the body in good football position.

The defensive players who serve as ball carriers must be encouraged to act as nifty ball carriers, using their best moves. They must also be encouraged to try to escape the tackler by spinning out of his grasp. But, again, I must emphasize that the cuts by the ball carrier should be flat, lateral or parallel to minimize violent contact.

The use of the hands to actually strike the blow and then grab the ball carrier is a very good approach to the teaching of tackling. It increases the safety factory by using the hand to strike and absorb the blow rather than the head and neck.

There is no question in my mind that this technique with its emphasis on body position, head and leg focus, and use of the hands is also the most efficient way to teach tackling.

5

Defending
The
Pass

TEAM ASPECT

The defensive teams that are good at defending the pass are those made up of players who play well together. In no other aspect of team defense is there a greater interdependence. Successful execution by the pass coverage men is, to a great degree, dependent upon effective pass rush. By the same token, the better the coverage men do their jobs forcing the quarterback to hold the ball, the better chance the rushers have of pressuring the quarterback. The better the rush, the better the coverage — the better the coverage, the better the rush — has been a fact of life in defensive football since the advent of the forward pass.

PASS RUSH

The goal of every pass rusher on every pass play is to get to the quarterback before he throws the ball. The sack is the ultimate reward or payoff for the effort expended by the rusher. Too many times, however, the evaluation of the effectiveness of the rush is only in terms of sacks. Rushing the passer is one technique in football where being close really does count. Even though the rusher may not tackle the quarterback before he throws the ball, his efforts often have a positive effect on the performance of the defense. As with the sack, a ball deflected by the raised hands and arms of the rusher is a pass that cannot be completed.

There are other positive results that can be achieved by a rusher who gets close to the quarterback and in front of him. This type of pressure may force the quarterback to hurry his pass or release the ball before he wants to, therefore affecting his accuracy. Pressure in front of the passer may also obstruct his vision, causing him not to see the receivers as they run their routes. A rusher in the face of the thrower can also force him to throw over the defender, thus causing the ball to be released with a higher trajectory. This causes the ball to be in the air longer, allowing the pass defenders more reaction time to the ball.

It is important that all players who are involved in rushing the passer understand all the objectives or goals involved. There are many times, for example, when teams are throwing pass patterns and actions with the passer dropping three or four steps. With these types of drops it is very difficult to get to the passer with the ball in his hands. However, the rushers can be effective if their rush puts them in front of the quarterback with their hands up.

Alignment

The pass rusher has to try to get to the edges or corner of the blockers as quickly as possible. The best way for him to do this is by his alignment. The wider a rusher can align, the greater his chances of being in a position to work off the corner of the pass protection. This is especially true for outside rushers, the defensive ends, or outside linebackers. The wider alignment forces the offensive man to compromise his squared-up relationship with the line, thereby increasing the chance he will cross his feet over, lose his power base, and his ability to adjust to moves. While the head-up alignment gives a rusher a clear two-way option, the fact that the blocker can set square or parallel to the line means that, in most cases, the rusher has to take the long route to the passer around the blocker.

Takeoff

Initial takeoff or the ability of the rusher to start on a movement by the offense is a critical factor in pass rush. The rusher's stance must be such that he is looking at the football but geared to go on any movement by the offense. Much of the time, the quarterback will jab step, or an offensive lineman will move his hand, just before the snap. Any of these types of pre-snap movements should trigger the rusher to move.

The burst by the lineman or linebacker on movement must be up the field or toward the offense, not up in the air. The rusher must gain as much ground as he can toward the offensive line of scrimmage on his initial steps. The key is to keep the head and shoulder level low and not raise up out of the stance on the initial movement.

There are two important issues here. One is that the offense knows when the ball is to be snapped. The defensive men can minimize this advantage by great initial takeoff. The second is that the offense is trying to establish a new line of scrimmage with their pass sets. This of course allows them more time to adjust to moves or pass-rush techniques by the defensive man. Again, the importance of initial takeoff by the defender to reduce the time the blocker has to adjust.

STRIKING A BLOW — POWER
OR LEVERAGE RUSH

Undoubtedly the quickest, shortest route to the quarterback is an unobstructed straight line. However, obstacles in the form of offensive blockers are usually in the paths of the rushers. Too many times the pass rushers assume that they need only finesse the blocker to beat him. It is a fact that there are times when moves and countermoves require very little contact with the offensive man but most of the time the blocker will have to be defeated before any type of pass rush move can be used.

On movement by the offense the rusher drives his hands forward, aiming for the outside upper tips of the front numbers on the blocker's jersey. It is important that all the movement of the hands and arms be forward. The aiming point is the tips of the numbers to ensure that the arc of the hands is inside the hands and arms of the blocker. The objective is to try to get both hands and arms on the inside; even if the rusher is successful in getting only one hand in this area, he can execute a number of pass-rush moves successfully. However if the offensive player is successful in getting both his hands inside those of the rusher, it is then very difficult to execute most rush techniques successfully.

The blow is struck with the palms and heels of the hands and must be delivered with enough power to force the offensive man backward or, at the minimum, shift his weight from the balls of his feet to the heels. This, of course, limits the blocker's ability to react quickly to changes of direction by the rusher. As the hands strike the blow, the elbows should lock, thereby bringing into use the additional force of the back muscles. It is important that the shoulder level of the rusher remain lower than that of the blocker at all times.

This ensures that the defensive man will have the big muscle or leverage advantage.

As the blow is struck it is important that the hands be open to strike with the palms and heels. However, right after this occurs, the rusher must grab the jersey or pads of the blocker to turn him. Again the most desirable place to rush from is over the corners of the blockers. I think, however, that the place to start teaching pass rush technique is with the leverage or power-rush position with both hands inside. Since this is the most difficult position to rush from, once a player understands the basic elements involved in beating the blocker from his head-up position, the techniques executed from other alignments are not as hard to acquire.

Takeoff should resemble a sprint to and around the blocker if a minimum of contact is required to beat the blocker. If, however, the rusher must bring into play all the elements of the power rush, he has to be able to get under control with quick, short, choppy steps. This enables him to change directions quickly as he power rushes or works to the corners of the blocker.

THE RUSH MOVE

All pass-rush moves over or through the blocker are some combination of push or of push, pull, and turn. From the leverage or head-up position it is desirable to drive the blocker back into the passer. This is especially true when the quarterback is using a short drop. With very little movement back the rusher is in a position to be a factor in front of the passer. However, this type of power rush is effective only in limited circumstances. Most moves that start as leverage rushes must ultimately involve speed or finesse over the corners or edges of the blockers to be successful.

By pushing with one hand and pulling with the other simultaneously, the rusher is accomplishing two things. One, he is turning the blocker and taking away the parallel relationship the blocker is trying to maintain with the line of scrimmage. When the pass protector can hold this position, he is forcing the rusher to take a long route around him to the passer. The other is that by turning the blocker he is exposing an edge or corner of the blocker to rush over.

If a rusher is going to make his move on the outside of the blocker off the power rush, he should pull with his outside hand and push with the inside. This push and pull turns the blocker and exposes the outside edge or corner of the blocker. As the pass protector is being turned, the rusher takes a big step with his inside leg as close to the blocker as possible. It is important that the rusher burst or accelerate past the blocker as he turns him. By rubbing close to the blocker, the rusher is staying on a direct course to the passer as well as reducing the time the protector has to recover.

How the rusher uses his off arm or the inside arm on an outside rush very often determines whether or not the passer is pressured effectively. There are two techniques that can be used here. One is the rip. With the rip-arm technique, the inside arm and shoulder are driven up and through the outside arm and shoulder of the blocker. The other is the swim or arm-over technique where the inside arm is thrown over the outside shoulder of the blocker much like the action used in freestyle swimming. It is important that the rip-arm and swim techniques be executed simultaneously with a pull with the other arm and a big step by the blocker. On inside rushes the pull is executed with the inside arm and the push and swim or rip with the outside arm. The shoulder level of the rusher must stay down all through the rush. I think the rip-arm action with the off arm should be taught first. With the rip technique the rusher is more likely to keep his shoulder level down. Use of the swim technique usually causes rushers to raise up and thereby compromise the leverage advantage.

After the rusher gets by the blocker, he has to get back under control with his feet moving in short, choppy steps. He must work to get in front of the passer. If the passer has the ball in his hands, the rusher should attempt to make a high tackle, driving his hands and arms through his throwing arm and shoulders. As the passer raises the ball to throw it, the rusher should extend his hands and arms, keeping his feet on the ground. If the rusher leaves his feet as the passer raises the ball, he is vulnerable to being finessed by a pump fake and allowing the passer to escape the sack. If the man rushing the passer is coached to keep his eyes focused on the numbers of the passer, he will be able to raise his hands and keep his feet on the ground as he finishes his rush.

The counter off the leverage or power rush involves engaging the blocker by striking a blow, faking either inside or outside, then rushing over the opposite corner of the blocker. With this move it is important that the man using the technique make every aspect of the move upfield or toward the blocker. In order for any rush to be effective, the blocker must be threatened by pressure at him. He must always feel a chance exists that the rusher will try to run over or power rush him. This causes the blocker to firm up or set stronger, which reduces his ability to move his feet quickly or adjust to moves by the rusher.

OUTSIDE OR GAP RUSHES

The quality most essential in an athlete if he is to pressure the passer from the outside is speed. There is no substitute for it. Initial quickness and technique can improve the effectiveness of a slower player, but without speed the potential for success at the defensive end or outside linebacker position is limited.

It is important that outside rushers line up with enough width to enable them, from a slightly pointed-in stance, to have a straight line to the passer. This angle or aiming point should be directly behind the center at the depth at which the quarterback normally sets to throw.

As in all rush techniques, initial takeoff with the ability to quickly gain ground upfield is critical. The rusher is literally trying to beat the offensive man out of his stance. The blocker has to be made to feel he has the threat of being beaten by the speed and quickness of the rusher around him outside. Thus the objective of the rusher is to sprint, in as straight a line as possible, to the passer. It really helps the rusher to aim just outside the tip of the offensive tackle's shoulder pads.

The rusher should reach to grab the outside arm and shoulder pad of the blocker, pulling himself and, at the same time, ripping the inside arm and shoulder to tighten or squeeze the angle.

The counter to the outside speed rush is the inside move on the blocker. Usually when a rusher establishes a hard upfield speed rush, the blocker tries to compensate by moving rapidly to the outside to block the rusher. This causes him to compromise his parallel relationship with the line of scrimmage, cross his feet over, and reduce his ability to adjust to an inside move.

It is important that the rusher be patient and not hurry his move. He should aim to get to the tip of the outside shoulder of the blocker before he makes the inside move. After he forces the blocker to cross over, the rusher should grab the inside arm or shoulder pad of the blocker with his inside hand and rip through the inside arm and shoulder of the blocker with his outside arm and shoulder.

I am convinced that all pass rush moves that are effective come off or utilize parts of, or all of, the elements described above. It is really important that coaches isolate those elements that are essential in good pass-rush technique, then continually demand that they be employed. The techniques may vary some but the basic elements of takeoff or initial quickness, elevation and pressure upfield, engaging the blocker or striking a blow, using the hands and feet and acceleration in the move, apply in virtually ever circumstance.

The elements of technique are described here as they apply to the drop-back pass. The pass sets by the pass protectors vary from firm on the line of scrimmage to soft, or with the blocker setting up to block as much as two or three yards back. The general rule is the firmer the set, the quicker the defender makes his move. The deeper the set, the further the rusher has to go to the blocker before he makes his move.

In play action or sprint-out passes, the same elements of technique apply. However, if aggressive blocking is being used, the application of the various aspects of pass rush occurs after the defender defeats the run blocker and he recognizes a pass play.

GAMES AND STUNTS

Games and stunts between linemen and linebackers can be effective aids to assist a defensive team in putting pressure on the quarterback. I believe they can be effective if these exchanges of rush lanes are used as changeups or as a surprise element. I also think they have to be run with a specific purpose in mind. For example, some stunts or games are better suited to use against teams whose basic protections dictate that they be blocked man-to-man. Others are more effective versus teams that pick up stunts and games with zone protection. Against teams that use deep drops with the quarterback, any number of games or stunts can be effective. However, with the three- or five-step-drop teams, things must be done quickly with the basic design aimed at getting quick pressure up the middle in the face of the passer.

There are a few basic and important rules to observe in executing pass rush games and stunts. The first is that if two men are executing a game or stunt together, the man who goes first must know whether or not the offense is blocking zone or man-to-man. If they are blocking zone protection, the man going first should try to grab or pull the man he is lined up over and take him out of the zone. He needs to stay close to the man he is pulling to open the lane for the second man. If man-for-man protection is used, the rusher going first should drive at an angle to pick or cut off the man assigned to block the second defensive man. It is very important that the second man in the stunt be patient and work forward or attack the offensive man he is lined up over before he comes around to exchange rush lanes with the man he is executing the game with. If he does a good job of flashing his opponent, this delay allows the first man to collapse the area or shorten the distance he has to go to get to the quarterback. The deeper the drop by the passer, the more the second man, whether it be a lineman or linebacker, can delay by threatening the straight ahead rush. Again, these games and stunts are most effective when they are used infrequently as changeups to the normal types of upfield pressure individual rushes. The element of surprise is an important factor.

6

Pass Coverage

The two basic types of pass coverage, zone and man-to-man, have the similar goals and objectives of preventing the opponent from completing passes. However they vary, by design, in the philosophical approach to pass defense. While the zone teams rely on the ability to defend areas of the field, the man-for-man teams challenge the receivers on an individual match-up basis and count on winning a high percentage of the one-on-one battles. In zone coverage the ball is the issue; in man coverages the man the individual defender is assigned to cover is the focal point. Zone teams expect that some short passes will be completed in front of or underneath the short defenders but that no deep passes will be completed. Conversely the man-for-man teams concede no completions. Where the problem comes, of course, is that if the individual matchups do not all hold up, and the passer is allowed to hold the ball long enough for a receiver to get open, a long completion becomes probable. The man-for-man concept of pass coverage does demand a more consistent type of pass rush and is based on a high percentage of the eleven defensive players winning the one-on-one rush or coverage battles most of the time.

Although the pass rush is important to zone teams, the ability of all defenders to break on the throw and converge on the ball goes a long way in determining their success. It is important to note here that zone teams are better equipped to involve the deep pass defenders in defending the run, because their focal points are the blocking schemes and the ball. This means that the defensive backs are in a good position to read and react to the run quickly. In man-to-man coverages each deep defender's focus must be totally on the man being covered, which means that many times the deep defenders have their backs to the line of scrimmage while covering receivers.

There is no question that zone and man-to-man types of pass coverage both have advantages and disadvantages in specific situations. Every good defensive team needs to be able to play some zone and some man-for-man coverage. It is, however, very clear to me, that a team must choose one type of coverage over the other as their primary pass defense scheme. There is no way a team can employ both zone and man coverages equally and reach a high enough level of proficiency to become a dominant defensive team. There is not enough practice and preparation time at any level of competition to allow as many repetitions as would be needed to place equal emphasis on both types of coverage.

PRE-SNAP READ

The ability of the defense to disguise the coverage they will play is, a very important factor in assisting the defense to execute. The care with which the pass defenders monitor their alignments, stances and any other factors that might tip the offense as to what coverage they are playing is one of the most critical factors in determining success in this area. For example, for a cornerback on a basic zone team to show a bump-and-run alignment on the first play being used on a man-for-man coverage is not wise. It does not make any sense to help the offense in this manner.

There are two general ways a team can disguise their coverage. Both are effective. One is to line up in the same pre-snap look or alignment on every play, whether a zone or man-for-man coverage has been called. The other is to vary the alignments on a continual basis. This forces the offense to guess whether a corner lining up in bump-and-run coverage means is he really covering the receiver man-for-man or, is he going to jam the receiver and defend the flat zone or at the last second, is he going to drop back and be a deep outside defender. No matter how it is done, disguising the coverage and not giving the offense a pre-snap read is important.

Players can be given a great degree of latitude in moving around to disguise the coverage. They do, however, need to be careful not to move around so much that they are not in a position to play their coverage responsibility when the ball is snapped.

ZONE PASS COVERAGE

When a coaching staff elects to become a zone team, they are selecting a way to play that requires patience and constant attention to detail. The ability to make subtle adjustments during each week of the season is very often the difference between success and failure with zone teams.

The simplest but least effective way to play zone coverages is to defend areas or spots on the field with little regard for other factors. For example, if the defender who is designated to defend the curl zone is asked only to get to an area two yards inside the numbers and read the quarterback, his assignment is not too difficult to execute. Likewise, if the deep defenders in a three-deep zone are coached only to drop, divide the field in thirds, and prevent the deep pass completion, chances are good that they could accomplish these things a high percentage of the time.

This type of coaching indicates to me a vision of defense as placing a priority on defending the field. I agree that to play zones effectively, areas of the field need to be defended — but they need to be defended only if there are offensive players in those areas in position to make plays.

This means that many other factors — such as down and distance; formations, including splits by receivers; pass patterns being run as well as the vertical position of the ball on the field — are all important, specific factors that determine how zone defenses are played. The lateral position of the ball on the field is not as significant a factor in professional football due to the placement of the hash marks. In high school and college football, with the hashes closer to the sideline, the position of the ball laterally is a greater factor in determining how zones are played.

Collapsing or Squeezing the Zones

It is very difficult to defend the field from sideline to sideline laterally, or vertically from one end to the other with zone coverages. There are not enough pass defenders available to fill all the areas where the offense could throw the ball. It is then clear to me that the defense must find ways to collapse or condense or squeeze the areas they have to defend. What this amounts to is the defense using all the information and specific factors they have at their disposal and applying them to defending only those areas or zones where there is the threat of a pass being thrown or completed. For example, if an offensive team employs a formation without a receiver split on a side, it does not make any sense to defend any more width than the immediate area outside the tight end on that side. The offense has, by its use of this formation, allowed the defense to collapse or squeeze the deep outside as well as the flat zone on that side. As the

pass play develops, the offense may force the defenders on that side
to defend more width but this will happen only with the development
of the pass pattern. Of course, if the defenders are coached to read
and react to patterns, they will adjust their width according to the
action by the offense. If the offense uses a formation with wide splits
by the receivers, they have stretched the lateral zones by this alignment.
However, the defense should be coached to understand that even though
these big splits would seem to force them to defend more width, these
wide splits also reduce the threat of out patterns by the wide receivers.
This means that the flat defenders do not need to be as concerned
about defending the out route as they do about stopping inside routes
by the wide split receiver.

As the pass patterns develop, whether or not a zone needs to
be defended with more or less width and depth depends on the
combination of routes used by the receivers. If an outside defender
sees the widest possible receiver work inside, he collapses or squeezes
as far as the route will allow him to. The big factor here is that the
defender must look for crossing receivers coming into his area as he
collapses. If there are none, he continues to collapse the zone.

Defining the Zones

In zone pass coverage, the field is divided into zones that become
the responsibility of a specific defender. These areas vary in width
and depth and are defined in more specific terms according to the
offensive formation. This is especially true in the short zones or those
that involve the underneath coverage men. I think it is very important
to be specific in coaching zone coverages. It serves no practical purpose
to designate more pass zones than are necessary. The more different
zones and terms the players are forced to learn, the less effective will
be their understanding of the basic concepts of carrying receivers
in zones.

The Short Zones

The short zones are those areas on the field that extend generally
from the line of scrimmage to a depth of ten to twelve yards. The
outside zone is the flat which stretches from the sideline to the outside
edge of the yard line numbers on a National Football League field.
The hook zones are those that extend from the middle of the formation
to the area slightly outside the tight end. If there is no tight end,
it extends from the middle to approximately three yards outside the
offensive tackle. The area between the flat and hook zones is defined

two ways. It is the curl zone if a receiver's route involves him turning in and working to an open spot. Curl zones may extend as deep as twenty-five yards. This area becomes a seam if the receiver continues up the field and runs through the area looking for the ball to his inside. The ability of short defenders to carry or cover the receivers in their zones to other zones is dependent upon the specific pass pattern being run. It is important that coaches, in describing zone responsibilities to the underneath coverage people, do so in terms of how their zones may expand or collapse according to their pattern read. For example, a hook defender should have his responsibility defined as hook to curl or seam. We are now telling the man responsible for the hook that if there is no receiver in the hook zone, but the ball is being thrown in the curl or seam areas, then it is his responsibility. If the man responsible for the flat is a linebacker or safety moving from the inside to cover the flat, his responsibility should be described as curl to flat. In other words, defend the curl until the flat is threatened. It makes no sense to drive to the flat if the offense does not have a threat there. This ability to hold off the curl before going to the flat also serves the purpose of giving the hook defender time to get to the curl. If the flat defender is a cornerback rotating up, his responsibility should be described as flat to curl. This means that as he rolls up and jams the wide receiver, he should collapse or squeeze. If he is not threatened in the flat, he should carry the receiver to the curl. Defining the zones in this manner, along with describing responsibilities in terms of progressions, facilitates players' learning to play the pattern read type of zone pass coverage.

The type of underneath zone coverage just described basically involves four defenders in four zones. If, however, the scheme makes available five defenders in underneath or short coverage, some adjustment needs to be made. With five defenders available in coverage short, the defense loses its balance. The extra man available can be used in many ways. The best way to use him is to say that there is now a defender available in the curl or seam areas and as a result the flat and hook defenders do not have to be concerned with collapsing or expanding. On the side of the defense where there are only two coverage people underneath, they play their normal hook to curl or seam and curl to flat coverage.

The Deep Zones

In the three-deep type of zone coverage, the field is divided in thirds from sideline to sideline. The two deep outside zones extend vertically from approximately 12 yards from the line of scrimmage to the opponent's goal line. Laterally or horizontally, the outside third zones are approximately 18 yards wide. Much like the short zones, they vary in width and are squeezed or collapsed by field position, the offensive formation and pattern run by the offense. The deep middle or post area extends vertically from approximately fifteen yards from the line of scrimmage to the goal line. Horizontally, it is the area between the two deep outside zones.

In the two-deep type of zone coverage, the deep defenders divide the field in half laterally. Vertically the amount of field they have to defend dictates that their alignment be deeper and as a result, their area of responsibility is from fifteen yards from the line of scrimmage to the goal line.

Intermediate Areas as Zones

The areas between the short and deep defenders are called the intermediate zones. They are created as the pass patterns develop and can occur at varying depths, starting at about fifteen yards from the line of scrimmage. The defending of these zones by the defense is dependent upon the short defenders reading patterns and covering receivers vertically through the deepest portions of zones and by the reaction of the deep defenders to what occurs in front of them.

READING THE QUARTERBACK

Where the quarterback looks and his throwing motion are two critically important factors in zone pass defense. The ability of the pass defenders to break or drive as the quarterback looks at a receiver or as the ball is thrown is the key to the defense making plays. All techniques taught should emphasize that the defenders drop as quickly as possible and be in a position anywhere in their drop to see the quarterback's action and drive at the ball. As the defender drops and reads the patterns, he must get his eyes focused on the passer.

The short defenders must break on the look of the passer. In other words, as soon as the passer looks at a receiver and starts his throwing motion, the hook and flat defenders must react.

Sometimes the quarterback looks and throws simultaneously. This does not occur very often. Most of the time the passer will look where he is throwing before he begins his throwing motion. There are a few isolated times when the passer will look off a defender by looking one way and throwing another but these are rare occasions and the defense can't let them affect how they play.

The deep defenders must have both actions by the passer occur before they break or drive on the receiver and ball. As the quarterback looks and throws the ball, the deep defenders break. The look-off by the passer can be fatal or result in six points if a deep defender is faked out of position. Since the ball is usually traveling further and is in the air longer, the deep defenders do not need to get as big a jump as the short defenders. If the short defenders are going to make plays on the ball, they must react to the look of the quarterback and anticipate the throw. It is very difficult for them to be effective if they are limited to reacting only when the quarterback actually throws the ball.

Reading Patterns

The look and throw of the passer are the indicators that allow the defenders to make plays in zone coverages. The direction in which the quarterback looks and his passing action give the coverage men the time-span keys that tell them when to break on the ball. Reading and reacting to the specific pass patterns run by the offense allow the defenders to tighten the coverage on the receivers who are in their zone. The specific patterns or combinations of pass routes determine the amount of width or depth a defender has to attain as he plays his zone responsibility. For example, if the number two receiver on the strongside, the tight end, releases straight up the field, then breaks outside, the hook defender on that side widens or expands. If the receiver is running an inside route, he covers him over the top to the middle of the formation. If the deep outside third defender has the wide receiver run an inside route, he collapses or carries him inside, until the number two man on that side runs an outside route or a crossing receiver threatens his area. If the halfback on the weak side releases wide outside, the defender stretches to the receiver running the curl.

Whether or not a defender plays a receiver in his zone as he reads the pattern depends on the action of the quarterback. If the passer is looking to the side of the defender, the defender must challenge the receiver in his zone. If the quarterback is looking away or the primary key in the pattern read blocks or goes across the formation, the defender reacts only to the look and throw of the quarterback. The tightening of coverage or clamping on receivers in zones takes place only if the passer is looking that way.

In addition, the pattern-read type of zone defense assures that the defense will always win the numbers game. That is, they will always have as many, and in most cases more, defenders available to cover in an area than the offense has receivers. When a receiver goes across the formation to overload a side, the defender reading him in the pattern read works to the overload side.

HORIZONTAL STRETCHES AND VERTICAL LEVELS

In addition to overloading zones, many teams attack zone teams by stretching the zones horizontally or laterally. The theory here is to open areas in which to throw the ball by forcing the defense to defend the width of the field. One of the ways one-back balanced teams do this is by releasing the wide receiver and tight end on each side up the field on deep routes. This forces the three deep defenders to defend the deep zones sideline to sideline. Unless the underneath defenders can help carry at least one of these receivers deep, there will be a seam open for the offense to throw the ball in. Another example of horizontal stretching is an inside or outside receiver releasing inside upfield, then breaking sharply outside. By releasing inside, they pressure the defender to collapse the zone inside and open an outside seam to throw the ball in. Although this horizontal stretching of zones creates some problems, the fact that the passer has only one receiver in the area where he is looking enables the defense to get a good jump on the ball.

One of the most effective ways to control the underneath coverage of zone teams is to throw pass patterns where the receivers operate at varying levels vertically. The theory here is to use a combination of receivers, usually two, who line up directly in the quarterback's line of sight. One of the receivers is deep, anywhere from fifteen to twenty yards, and the other operates under the drop of the short defender. These patterns are designed to give the passer a specific defender to read. If, for example, the hook defender has a deep-in route by a wide receiver behind him and a circle or hook route by a back in front of him, he is forced to make a decision as to which one he will cover. Since the receivers are in a straight line vertically, the look of the quarterback is of little value to him in determining which one the quarterback is throwing to. Experience in reading these types of patterns, the trajectory and velocity of the pass, are all factors that help the defender make plays on these types of patterns. The rule — when in doubt cover the deepest receiver — applies here but the ability to make a play on the ball in this difficult read situation is characteristic of good zone teams.

DROPS

The pass drops of the linebackers in zone coverages are crucial in determining how well they play pass coverage. This is especially true because they must move away from the line of scrimmage, yet be in a position in a short time to react in every direction. As soon as they read pass, they begin their drop by opening their hips and driving toward their zone responsibility. It is important that as they turn their hips to drop, they keep their shoulder level down and stay as parallel as possible to the line of scrimmage. By not raising their shoulder level, they are better able to gain distance quickly on the drop and not lose time by raising up out of their stance. On the first few steps of the drop, they need to be able to see their primary read and then focus back on the passer for three-step drop. If the quarterback drops only three steps and throws, the short defender must break flat toward the receiver to whom the ball is being thrown.

After clearing three-step drop by the quarterback, the defender continues his drop, reading the pattern as he goes. It is important that as the quarterback sets to throw, the defender's feet are under him, and he is in position to break on the ball. I do not think keeping the shoulders parallel all through the drop can be overemphasized. By dropping with the shoulders parallel, the defender's head and eyes are facing the line of scrimmage enabling him to read patterns as he drops, as well as focus on the quarterback and his action.

BREAKING ON THE BALL

Teams that play zone defenses well do not allow deep passes to be completed against them. They force the offense to throw passes in front of the short defenders. How well a team defends or reacts to the short pass is very often a factor in determining whether or not it can keep its commitment to playing zone coverages. If a team does not handle this part of the game well, four-yard completions turn into eight-yard gains. The answer to controlling the underneath passing game lies in how the short defenders react to the ball. A defender who knows how to react to a ball thrown in front of him is one who understands the value of good pass-drop technique. He also has good ability to read patterns and understands the importance of driving on the receiver at good angles. If a ball is to be caught in front of a short defender, he must drive on the receiver with a high degree of velocity. He has to always be aware of the shoulder he is going to make the hit with or in other words the angle at which he will drive to make the tackle. The application of a simple rule is the best assurance that this will happen. If a ball is caught in front of a defender but to his inside, he drives to make the tackle with his inside shoulder. If a catch is made outside, he drives to make the hit with his outside shoulder. The application of this simple rule eliminates any doubt in the mind of the defender and assures high velocity drives on the ball. In other words, four-yard passes do not become eight-yard gains.

They either become incomplete passes because of the high velocity contact made or at best are four-yard gains. Zone teams can live with short completions but they cannot stay in zone coverages all the way down the field if the offense can turn relatively short passes into big gains. Knowing how to drive on the ball with the proper angle is the confidence factor that short defenders need to counter the way most offensive teams attack good zone coverages.

SCREENS

The screen pass is one of the types of passing actions used most frequently to attack zone teams. The theory behind the high frequency of screen against zone is that while the short defenders are dropping, the screen has the time to develop. It is very important that zone teams assign specific responsibilities to defend the various types of screens.

Quick or hitch screens require that the cornerback on the side of the pass drives from the outside in and makes the tackle with his inside shoulder pad. The flat defender drives inside out and makes the hit on the receiver with his outside shoulder pad.

Slow-developing screens designed to be run outside by backs or tight ends are all defended the same way. The defender responsible for the flat is the outside man, and he drives to make the tackle with his inside pad. The hook defender drives from the inside out making the tackle with his outside pad.

On middle screens, the hook defenders drive on the ball, making the hit with the inside shoulder pad.

It is important for players reacting to screens to know they will have to play off blockers before they will be able to execute their responsibilities. The ability of the defenders to use their hands in working off blockers determines whether or not screens can be stopped by zone teams.

I believe in employing zone coverages as a base way to play pass defense. With the pattern-read type of zone coverage, coaching the zones is a constant challenge. The pattern reads can vary from week to week but the basic philosophy and techniques do not. Playing zones requires commitment, patience, and continuous coaching and attention to detail. However, if preventing the score is the most important goal of a defensive team, there is no better way to play.

7

Man
Coverages

The simplest type of coverage from an assignment point of view is man-for-man coverage. It is the least complicated in theory but at times can be the most difficult to execute. For example, to indicate to a cornerback that his job is to cover a wide receiver man-for-man is not a very hard assignment to understand. It could, however, be very difficult to execute if the receiver runs a lot faster than the defender and the quarterback gets time to throw the ball deep. This type of coverage really does require matching athletic ability and skill. Man coverage also puts a greater demand on the rush since it is a fact that if the quarterback is allowed to hold the ball long enough, most receivers can get away from the man covering them and get open. There is no question this is why to play man coverages well it is so critical that the defense must assert pressure on the quarterback. Games, stunts, and additional linebackers committed to the rush are all ways people who run man-for-man coverages get additional pressure on the quarterback.

MATCHUPS

One of the key factors in utilizing man-for-man coverages is to keep the individual defenders matched up as closely as possible from an ability standpoint. It is important that coaches do not ask defenders to cover receivers whose athletic skills are much greater than their own. This is not only unreasonable but is also setting the stage for disaster. If these types of mismatches occur, the coach has the responsibility to do something to aid the defender. The first thing available is to increase the probability of pressure on the quarterback.

This can be done by games, stunts, or rushing additional defenders. The other option is to give him coverage help in the way of a free safety or double coverage help. It makes no sense for coaches to be aware of coverage mismatches yet do nothing about them, thereby exposing their team to the probability of big plays in the passing game.

Adjustments built into a scheme are important in this area. For example, when an offensive team lines up in a slot formation, placing both wide receivers on the same side, lining up both cornerbacks to cover them creates the best match-up situation from an athletic ability point of view. When a team chooses to do this, it helps with the matchup but it does force the inside corner on the slot side to learn how to play the assignment of the strong safety against the run. It also causes the outside man on the other side, the safety, to have to learn to play that cornerback position. I think whether or not to flip the corners depends on the basic pass defense philosophy of a team. I feel man-for-man teams should flip the corners, but zone teams should not.

Pressure on the passer is indeed a huge factor in determining success or failure in the utilization of man coverages. It is, therefore, a viable option to use any pass defender, not needed to cover a specific man, as a pass rusher. An example of this would be a man-for-man coverage where one or more of the linebackers is not assigned a specific man to cover. The availability of another rusher increases the chances of putting pressure on the quarterback and decreases the time receivers have to get open.

Another option in using a defender who does not have a specific man responsibility is to use him as a free safety. This, of course, is combining the deep middle defender aspect of zone defense with man-for-man defense. I like this option since it provides some of the same safety features as three-deep zone defenses. A man-to-man defense with a free safety provides the tight coverage possibilities of challenging receivers but with the security of a free safety to prevent the deep completion down the middle. This is especially important when there is a threat of poor matchups like a linebacker covering a fast back. If the quarterback reads this coverage and throws deep, it could be a touchdown with no free safety help. With a safety in the middle, there is a good chance that although the receiver may beat his man deep, the passer will not throw the ball into free safety coverage.

The other option to employ the defender without specific man coverage is to use him to double cover with another defender on a specific receiver. I think this is a good option, especially when linebackers are forced to cover receivers who are superior from an athletic standpoint. For example, if an outside linebacker is asked to force on running plays and cover a tight end man-for-man on passing plays, I think this is an unrealistic set of responsibilities. If, however, he is asked to do these things, but is assured double coverage help by another defender, then I think he has a good chance to execute at a high level.

Another option is to use freed-up defenders to zone off areas of the field or play a specific short zone in a man coverage. The theory is that the zone defender is available to help should a receiver get away from the man covering him. This is good in theory but the practicality of it is questionable. I really believe that in order for a man-for-man defender to be able to count on help, he has to know that it is there and constant and that he can count on it. If this is the case, the man defender can adjust his alignments and modify his techniques accordingly. If, however, the man he is counting on for help is forced to cover another receiver or misreads the quarterback or pattern, the potential for a big offensive play is great. To me, possible help on a receiver by a defender is worse than no help at all, since in the latter situation, the man coverage defender will put all his efforts into the personal challenge the type of coverage demands.

The most effective types of man-for-man coverage are those that combine the three elements. I am convinced that playing with a free safety in man coverages is the soundest way to play. I also think that the ability to rush with an additional linebacker combined with changeups that involve doubling specific receivers with freed-up cover people is the proper blend of variations. I do not like the option of the defender who is free in man coverage zoning off. The uncertainties of this type of coverage make it high risk and by using it, the defensive team compromises its margins.

THE MAN — THE ISSUE

In zone pass defense, the ball is the primary concern to the defenders, with the man catching it secondary in importance. Man coverages demand that the defenders focus primarily on the receiver. Playing the ball is important but in no way can the defender lose his focus on the receiver to look for the ball before the receiver makes his final cut.

The ball becomes the issue after it is in the air. The ability of the defender to close on the receiver and the ball is crucial to making plays in man coverages. After the receiver has made his final cut, the defender must drive to make a play on the ball at its highest point. If a defender is covering a receiver from a trail position or a location behind the receiver, he must keep his full concentration on the hands of the receiver. As the receiver adjusts to catch the ball, the defender must drive his closest hand and arm through the "pocket" the receiver makes to catch this ball. If the defender is able to reach the receiver quickly enough and has good tight coverage position, he can intercept the ball by scooping the ball out of the pocket with his inside arm.

It is important that pass defenders be coached with the idea that the ball is as much theirs as it is the receiver's once it is in the air.

Once the ball is in the air it belongs to the guy who wants it the most or is in the best position to catch it. The coverage man has as his primary objective the goal of intercepting every thrown ball. When he cannot do this, the next most important objective is to prevent the completion by deflecting the thrown ball.

However, there are times when the receiver gets his hands on the ball and makes it appear that the pass will be completed. It is in these situations that pass defenders have the opportunity to establish their physical presence in the game. If players are coached to go through the receiver and fight the receiver for the ball until the whistle blows, receivers will spend as much time looking for defenders as they will looking for the ball. The collisions that occur when a defensive back or linebacker drives through a receiver are always effective. Even if the hit does not cause the pass to be incomplete, the receiver will remember it the next time he runs a pass route.

Man Coverage Technique

Secondary Defenders

There are two basic positions or alignments secondary defenders use on receivers they are covering man-for-man. One is the off position which is the same pre-snap alignment used in all coverages. This is approximately one yard outside, and about seven yards deep. As the receiver moves downfield, the defender must gain a position on him, when he has free safety help inside, about a yard outside, and three yards off him. This outside position is desirable on deep patterns when free safety help can be counted on. On short and intermediate routes, the defender must stop any inside cuts by gaining an inside position or playing the ball through the receiver.

If he does not have help inside, as in blitz coverages, he must gain a tight inside shoulder position two yards off the receiver. It is important that the defender work to these positions in his backpedal and that he keep his full concentration on the numbers of the receiver.

The coverage man must develop the ability to judge the speed of the receiver as they release downfield, in order to establish and maintain the desired cover position. It is important that the defender drive on the first break as the receiver releases up the field. After he has achieved his position, he keeps his total concentration on the man until the ball is thrown.

Bump and run or press coverage is used most often with goal-line or blitzing types of defenses. With this type of coverage, the defender takes an alignment tight on the receiver with his outside foot between the numbers of the man he is covering. The defender must hold the inside position. He cannot take any inside fakes. The receiver must be made to release outside. The defender must use his hands on the receiver to force him outside. As the receiver releases downfield, the defender maintains a position approximately one yard inside and one yard behind him. Total concentration is on the receiver and the only time the defender looks for the ball is when the receiver adjusts his hands and eye level to make the catch. Occasionally, the outside bump-and-run technique is used but this is only when inside coverage help is available.

It is critical that the inside position be maintained whenever a coverage calls for it. There are two reasons why this position can never be lost by the defender. The highest percentage passes by quarterbacks are on inside routes. The catches are easier for the receivers, and the ball has less distance to travel than it does on outside routes. When the ball is thrown on outside routes, there is the additional factor that the receiver is going away from the passer while he is making the catch, which, along with the distance factor, adds to the degree of difficulty.

Linebackers

Linebackers are usually asked to cover running backs in man-for-man coverages. On occasion, they cover tight ends but this does not occur very often. In fact, I feel very strongly that because of all the other responsibilities assigned linebackers, they should not be asked to cover tight ends without help.

There is one principle that applies to all linebackers covering all backs and that is they must attack the man they are covering. They cannot wait on the defensive side of the line of scrimmage and allow the receiver two-way options in their routes. As soon as the linebacker recognizes pass, he must drive to junction the receiver on the offensive side of the line of scrimmage on all downfield releases. The defender works for an inside coverage position, forcing the outside release of the back. As he establishes this position, he must drive his inside foot upfield and inside the receiver. His outside foot should be approximately in the center of the man. As he gains this inside position with his foot, he uses his hands and arms to change the direction or release of the back. The outside hand is driven for the tip of the outside number on the receiver's jersey. The inside hand makes contact with the inside half of the receiver. He must concentrate and focus on the numbers of the receiver. As the defender makes contact, he is striving to establish the inside position as well as force the receiver to change his route. It is important that the linebacker keep his feet moving in short, quick steps all through the execution of this technique. This enables him to better react and change direction.

The defender must maintain good balance, with the weight distributed over the balls of his feet. He has to think more in terms of catching or absorbing than of striking. If he gets too intent on striking a big blow, he will lunge at the receiver, increasing the chances of his getting beat on an option route. The inside position is important to linebackers for the same reasons defensive backs play in this manner.

If the back releases in a wide arc, the linebacker must adjust his route to the receiver. As the back swings wide, the defender flattens his route and sprints to the inside of the receiver. It is very important that the angle is always inside out, striving to junction the receiver at his inside shoulder. The inside body position assures that the receiver cannot get back inside under the defender on an option route. If the receiver turns upfield, the defender gains the one-yard-inside and one-yard-trail position on him.

If the man he is assigned to cover blocks, the coverage man must physically attack the receiver. This hug technique is executed by attacking with the hands and gaining the inside position with the inside foot, similar to the way it is done with the junction or catch. As with the jam technique, we are taking the inside release away by body position. This technique of attacking helps to defend against screens since the aggressive hug technique allows the defender to get behind the blockers and stop the screen before it gets started. I do not favor using defenders whose man-coverage responsibility blocks to free up or zone off because of the problem screen passes can cause. If the defender does not attack on the blocking action by the receiver, when he does see the screen develop, it will be too difficult to stop since the blockers will be set up between him and the man running the screen. By using this technique, the defensive man avoids getting beat on any kind of delayed inside release by the back. Outside or middle screens and checkdowns are not problems in man coverages if the defenders are coached to hug the receivers when they block.

Double-Covering Receivers

One of the most effective ways to take a receiver away from an offense is to assign two defenders to cover him. Double coverage can involve any combination of pass defenders. It can involve two linebackers, two secondary men, or a linebacker and a safety or cornerback. Two defenders can double-cover a receiver by bracketing or coning him. This technique involves one defender covering the receiver from an inside position and the other outside. When this type of double coverage is used, it is important that the defenders keep enough distance between them and the receiver to prevent losing their inside or outside positions. When a receiver who is double-covered in this manner releases downfield and breaks inside, the inside defender drives on the cut. The outside coverage man holds his outside position with depth, anticipating a double cut by the receiver. If the receiver releases downfield and breaks outside on his initial cut, the outside defender drives on it, and the inside coverage man protects against the double cut. If the receiver's initial release is flat or parallel with the line of scrimmage, he is covered by the defender assigned to cover him in the direction he releases. The other defender frees up and zones off, keying the quarterback and reacting to his look and throw. It is important that the free defender be alert and prepared to give help on the receiver if he comes back inside off a flat outside release and vice versa. The double cut by the receiver is one of the biggest problems with this type of double coverage. There is also the danger of the receiver splitting this type of double coverage.

In addition to inside-outside double coverage, receivers can also be double-covered short and deep. With this type of coverage the short defender plays under or behind the receiver and the deep man plays deep or on top of him. The most effective way to play this type of coverage is to have the short defender jam the receiver and disrupt his release and route. I also feel the short defender must have inside coverage responsibility with the deep defender having the additional responsibility of outside route coverage.

Double coverage on receivers is a must whenever the athletic ability or the alignment of a receiver puts a single defender in a disadvantageous position. As mentioned previously, it is also a valuable aid when an outside linebacker is asked to cover a receiver man-for-man and force the run, especially in running downs.

8

Nickel
Defenses

The development of the nickel defense became necessary in professional football to counter the sophisticated pass offenses that were being devised. The utilization of three and four receivers in offensive formations made it necessary for the defense to devise ways to counteract these sets. The addition of the fifth or sixth defensive back enabled teams to better match-up with the receivers in the offensive formation. By adding the third or fourth receiver, the offenses increased the flexibility and overall effectiveness of the passing game. However, since the additional receivers replaced tight ends or running backs in the formation, their absence limited the running game. As a result, without a strong running threat, the defense could replace linebackers with defensive backs, and run-oriented defensive linemen with pass rushers.

RUSH

The pass rush aspect of nickel defenses is the area that really determines how successful nickel defenses are. It is important that pass rushers, in most cases defensive linemen, are coached to rush the passer and react to the run. In other words, their total concentration is on upfield pass rush. If rushers are to be effective and utilize the advantages they have, they cannot be limited by worrying about defending the run. Everything the rusher does — from his stance, takeoff, leverage position, and so on — is aimed at pressuring the passer. If a running play should develop, he has to react to it as best he can.

In most cases, the offense is in a long yardage situation when

the nickel defenses are employed. Most teams do not display the type
of confidence in their running game from passing formations to use
it with any degree of regularity. The runs are limited by formations
and usually consist of draws or traps with an occasional outside run.
The lack of a power side of the formation due to the absence of a
tight-end blocker, is probably the most significant factor in limiting
the run.

If the pass rushers are effective in penetrating the offensive line
of scrimmage as they rush, they disrupt the blocking scheme on runs.
The rushing linemen create the same type of defense against the run
as do blitzing and stunting types of defenses. Another factor in stopping
the run is that the nickel personnel on the field are playing in the
scheme because they can run fast, which is the prerequisite to good
pursuit against the running game. As a result, the pursuit ability
of nickel teams is usually better than that of the team's regular
personnel.

Nickel alignments allow the defense to expand the type and
number of coverages they run. Since the additional defensive backs
should match up well with the receivers, the biggest variety occurs
in the man-for-man coverages. When personnel other than the fifth
and sixth defensive backs are used, the types of man coverages a team
can use are limited. This is due to the coverage mismatches that can
occur in some coverages that do not exist when a defensive back
assumes the coverage of a linebacker. I prefer the alignment that
employs six defensive backs. With this alignment the sixth defensive
back, or dime back as he is often called, is available to play the coverage
normally assigned to a nickel linebacker. In most cases this means
the dime back has a chance to be dominant in athletic ability over
the receiver he is usually assigned to cover in man-for-man defenses.

UTILIZATION OF PERSONNEL

The defensive teams that are the best equipped to play these
types of defenses well have three players with the cornerback type
of coverage ability. Both corners, and the man playing the nickel back
position, need to be this kind of athlete. The safeties are usually the
same personnel who play in all situations. Although they may not
possess as much speed as the cornerbacks, they must be good athletes
and have the ability to cover wide receivers man for man. The sixth
defensive back or the man in the dime linebacker position should be
this same type of player from a coverage standpoint, but be physical
enough to play the run from a linebacker's alignment. The player
in the other linebacker position needs to be the linebacker on the team

who has the best man-for-man coverage ability. This player is also, in most cases, the fastest of this group.

The defensive ends or outside rushers should be the defensive linemen who run the fastest. Although technique is very important, the ability to run fast is the single most important asset a defensive end can have. There is no substitute for it.

The inside rushers or tackles can rely more on strength, but they do need to have the ability to change directions quickly. The counter to power-rush techniques is quick moves to the corners of the blockers, and those who are quick as well as strong are best equipped to be effective. Speed is never a liability at any of the positions on the defensive team.

ALIGNMENTS

Coverage Men — Pre-snap Read

It is important that the coverage men in the nickel defense do not give away the coverage by their alignment. They must disguise the coverage by aligning in the same position on all coverages or vary their alignments in such a fashion as not to give the offense a pre-snap read. It is important that the coaching staff demand a specific pre-snap alignment on every play, especially early in the teaching process. After a while, it may be permissible to allow them the latitude to change their alignments.

Depth

The two best alignments from a depth standpoint are to have the cornerbacks, nickel, and two safeties lined up seven to eight yards deep. From this position they can play all coverages, man-for-man, zone, or blitz. The other is to align all the deep defenders within five yards of the line of scrimmage and either blitz or drop and execute their coverage responsibilities from this depth. It is important to give offensive teams the latter look because it is a better position for the deep defenders to blitz from. Since many offensive teams call an audible or automatic to their blitz adjustments when the deep defenders are lined up within five yards of the line of scrimmage, to show this alignment and then play normal coverages can create problems for the opponent's passing game in the way of indecision on the part of the quarterback and the receivers. Both types of five-across alignments are necessary. The deeper alignment places defenders, especially the safeties, in a better position to execute their responsibilities in most coverages. As mentioned earlier, the closer alignment is better to blitz from.

Lateral Positions

The corners are the wider defenders on each side. The nickel back is the inside defender on the strong side and usually lines up over the inside or number two receiver. If a team is using three receivers in the game, the nickle is usually aligned in this position. If there is a tight end in the formation on his side he aligns outside him. The nickel back must be in a position to execute the same run force responsibilities as the strong safety does in normal defenses.

The strong safety lines up in a position approximately opposite the area normally occupied by the tight end. The free safety lines up over the weak side offensive tackle.

Linebacker and Dime Back Positions — Pre-snap Read

Normal alignment for these positions is approximately three yards deep and laterally lined up opposite the man being covered in a man-to-man defense. Since one or the other of these players is dogging or blitzing frequently, the most effective changeup in their alignment is to threaten to blitz through a gap. As with the defensive back, however, it is important that by moving around in this fashion they do not compromise their chances of being able to get to the ball carrier on running plays or executing their pass coverage responsibility on pass plays.

Due to the fact that most offensive teams usually line up their best receiver of the backs on the weak side of the formation, this is where the dime back aligns. Since this man has defensive-back type of coverage abilities, he should be the best equipped of the short defenders to play this position. With a defensive back playing here, it is more difficult for the offense to force the defense into poor matchups man-for-man on the number two receiver on the weak side, as could occur when two linebackers are used as the short defenders. The fourth wide receiver in a formation is not the problem he would otherwise be if a defensive back were not used in this position. If a linebacker is assigned man-for-man coverage and the number two receiver on that side is a wide receiver, in most cases a defensive team is forced to change or modify their coverage. With a defensive back in this position, no changes are necessary. So here again the value of using a dime back is evident.

Front Four Defensive Linemen

The balanced even-front defense places a rusher over both guards and tackles. With an inside and outside rusher on each side, the objective is to collapse the pocket on the passer. The general goal of the tackles is to force the passer back and that of the defensive ends is to force him to step up. It is very important that the tackles get pressure in front of the passer, especially when the offensive design employs short drops by the quarterback.

The tackles must be conscious of the threat of a quick running play up the middle. Although they do not allow this threat to slow down their pass rush, one of them must adjust his alignment so he can better react to a run should one occur. The ends cannot be limited to outside rush lanes exclusively. They must be given the latitude to make inside pass rush moves. The mobility of the quarterback as well as whether or not the opponent is a rollout or sprint-out team are factors in determining how committed to the outside the defensive ends have to be. If there is a tight end in the formation, it is important that the defensive end align slightly to the tight end's inside, forcing the tight end to block down on outside runs, giving the secondary men a good, quick run key. If the defensive end aligns too tight to the offensive tackle and allows him to reach or overblock him, this allows the tight end to block the nickel back. This type of physical mismatch cannot be allowed to occur. It can be eliminated by the alignment of the end.

The even alignment, in addition to balancing the four man straight rush, creates equal game, stunt, and blitz threats on both sides. However, it does make the execution of games involving three linemen more difficult due to the distance the third man has to go to be involved.

Overs and Unders

The movement of a defensive tackle over the offensive center creates an overshift or undershift depending on whether or not he moves to the strong or weak side of the formation. These alignments are effective because they not only force the center to become a man-for-man pass protector, but they also force the offensive guards to block man for man without the possibility of quick help from the center. It is a good way to isolate a rusher on a specific offensive player. Overs and unders also cause the offense to make adjustments in their run blocking, especially the quick trapping game in the middle.

Games involving three men are more effective because the man over the center is in a better position to be involved.

The defensive ends align just as they do in the even front and execute the same responsibilities. If there are no games or stunts involved, the tackle over the center becomes the inside rusher away from the overshift. The other tackle must have the option of using an inside or outside move on the guard he is lined up over.

Three Defensive Linemen

There is some value in changing the personnel used in nickel or dime defenses. An effective way to do this is to replace a defensive tackle with a middle linebacker in the alignment. All other personnel remain the same and align in their usual positions. The tackle that remains in the game lines up over the offensive center and the middle linebacker stacks behind him. If four rushers are used, the nose tackle rushes to his right or left depending on the call he gets from the middle linebacker. The middle linebacker becomes the fourth rusher in this alignment and is responsible for the inside rush lane opposite the one the nose takes.

This is a simple but effective way to change the rush alignment. The nose tackle and middle linebacker are responsible for the same rush lanes the two tackles have in the four-man-line alignments. In addition, it also creates numerous opportunities for variations by involving the middle linebacker in coverage and rushing the other linebacker or dime. There are additional possibilities of rushing three linemen, involving both linebackers and the dime in coverage or blitzing all three of them on the same play.

COVERAGE SCHEMES

One of the most important factors in designing nickel coverages is that there must be carryover from the pass defense schemes used in regular defenses. There should be a similarity in the way the coverages are called, the way they are played, and the individual techniques required. Along these lines, the personnel used in the nickel defenses should be asked to execute as close as possible the responsibilities they assume in regular defenses. For example, the cornerback position is constant in both types of defense and as a result, there is great carryover from the regular scheme to the nickel. The corners are asked to play deep outside or rotate up, jam a receiver, and play the flat in regular zone defenses and nickel zones. In man-for-man or blitz coverages, they are basically covering the outside receiver on their side in both defensive schemes.

The safety positions in the nickel are similar in responsibilities to what they are in regular defenses. In the zones, they are deep half, deep middle, deep outside, or flat defenders in the nickel as well as in the regular defenses. The nickel back must learn to execute many of the same responsibilities strong safeties have in regular defenses. In a strong-zone type of coverage, he must learn to hold off the curl and defend the strong flat. In man-for-man schemes, he has coverage on the second receiver lined up on the strong side. Since the man best equipped to play this position from a physical ability standpoint is a cornerback, he does have some new learning situations.

The man who plays in the linebacker position is able to execute many of the same techniques and responsibilities he does in the regular defenses. In man-for-man coverages, he covers backs out of the backfield, and in the zones he is a hook or flat defender. There is plenty of carryover and the new learning is minimal.

It is a much different situation with the dime linebacker. For this defensive back who is playing in a linebacker position, much of what he is asked to do is not consistent with techniques he uses as a defensive back in regular defenses. Because he is lining up so much closer to the line of scrimmage, he has to learn to play against the run at different angles than he does playing as a defensive back. He also has to learn to cover receivers out of the backfield, which is different from what he is accustomed to doing as a defensive back in regular defenses. The dime running stunts and blitzing from the linebacker alignment are also new things he must learn to execute. It is important that practices be organized with time allotted for the dime linebacker to work with the linebackers on these specifics.

Coverage Variations

The complete nickel coverage package needs to have as its base a blend of zone, man-for-man, and blitz coverages. Although all teams that play nickel defenses have the capacity to run any coverage, most have a small number of coverage variations that they employ much more than others. One of the reasons nickel coverages were devised was to better match up defensive personnel with offensive players in man-for-man defenses. However, the increased use of the nickel defense has necessitated the use of zone coverages as part of the coverage scheme. These additional variations also reduce the predictability factor and make it more difficult for the offense to anticipate specific coverages.

Man-for-Man Coverages

Nickel man-for-man coverages usually fall into one of several different groups. One of these is the man-for-man coverage that utilizes a free safety. In this type of coverage the strong or free safety is a deep post defender and the remaining coverage people are committed to coverage. At times some type of five-man pass rush may be used, which means the short defender who does not have a specific man to cover blitzes and becomes the additional rusher. Another way to use the freed-up defender is to use him as a zone defender in an area of the field rather than blitz him. The defender who does not have specific man-for-man coverage plays zone and is assigned to be the extra defender on the strong or weak side. He may also be used as a rover defending the intermediate zone on both sides of the formation. The two-deep type of man-for-man coverage is another way to play man-for-man defense in the nickel. Both safeties defend deep half zones with the remaining pass coverage men all playing man-for-man coverage. Whenever a man is a zone defender in a base man-for-man defense, he must key the quarterback and break on his look and throw.

Another type of man coverage involves combinations of defenders covering receivers. These range all the way from two defensive players covering one receiver all over the field to a combination of defenders covering receivers based on their pass release.

The other type of man-for-man coverage is blitz coverage, which means that some of the pass defense players are committed to rushing the passer. This means that the remaining pass coverage men play man-for-man coverage on the receivers with no help. There is a big dependence on the rush whenever blitzes are used.

Zone Coverages

There are many situations when zone coverages are more appropriate than man for man. In very long yardage situations, two-minute situations as well as any time when the run is highly probable, zone defense is a useful part of the nickel coverage package.

Three-deep zone with four rushers is a very effective way to play the nickel defense. It is also possible to rush the passer with three linemen and use eight defenders in coverage. The three-defensive-linemen defense with three linebackers in the game provides the necessary personnel to play this particular coverage.

Two-deep zone coverage is a good changeup coverage used in conjunction with a three-deep zone. Both safeties are responsible for the deep half zone with the corners jamming the wide receivers and playing the flat zone. The linebacker and dime back are hook zone defenders much like they are in the sting zone. The nickel back plays the number two receiver on the strong side man for man all over the field.

Playing the number two receiver strongside, man-for-man, eliminates the possibility of getting him through the post area, splitting the two-deep zone. Covering him man for man also takes the number two receiver strongside out of the pattern read and enables the hook and flat defenders on both sides to read weak side patterns. Two-deep zone defense in the nickel package goes well when used in conjunction with two-deep man defenses in that the quarterback, on his initial read, has difficulty telling the difference between the two.

Defensive coaches must be careful to resist the temptation to include many different coverages in their nickel package — with the result being that the team does not become efficient at playing any of them. I am convinced a team is well-equipped with a few coverages that they know how to play effectively. Just as with coverages in regular defenses, it is impossible to be good at everything.

9

Practice Organization

I believe there are two general types of football practices. One is the pre-season or spring ball type where the basic goals are the development of skills and techniques and the teaching and learning of a defensive scheme. There is very little attention paid to specific game or opponent preparation in this type of practice. The focus is on the "home" team. The other type of practice is centered around specific game preparation. The primary goal here is to zero in on the opponent — what they do offensively and the defensive plan needed to stop them. Although it is very difficult to commit a high percentage of practice time to individual technique in the latter type of practice, a certain amount of technique work must be done in every practice. The inevitable result of not allowing time for technique work is a deterioration in execution.

It is the responsibility of the coaching staff to focus on specific areas that will be worked on in each practice. These specifics may apply to individuals, segments such as the defensive line, or the defensive team as a whole. It is important that the players be made aware of which areas are to be emphasized. I believe the players who improve their play the most are those who begin each practice with the goal of getting better in the execution of a specific skill. If a player can come off the field each day having improved his play in some way, his overall level of performance will inevitably increase.

Tempo is the speed or velocity or intensity with which a team practices. Teams that practice hard play games hard or with great effort and as a result, win. Coaches set the tempo for practice by

establishing standards and demanding that they be met. If, for
example, it is important that every defender break on the ball every
time it is passed, then the coaches should indicate this to the team
and demand that they do it on every play. It is especially important
that the tempo be monitored throughout the duration of the practice.
Hustling and playing with velocity is much easier early in practice
when the players are fresh than late when they are tired. I believe
they become what they are in games by the way they practice, and
it is the coach's responsibility to motivate them to work at a high
level at all times.

Practices do not have to be long to be productive; a plan must
be developed for each practice. This practice plan should include
a list of the things that are to be accomplished and the time frame
in which this is to be done. I believe in short practices as much
as is practical; I do not believe longer practices are as much a potential
problem in the pre-season as they are in the regular season. In
addition to the physical fatigue factor, the longer the players are
on the field the harder it is for them to concentrate. When they
lose their concentration, they make more mental errors and practice
becomes less productive.

Long practices usually occur as a result of poor planning or
a coach's frustration. Although coaches should set their goals high
regarding what they expect to accomplish in practice, they must
also be realistic and flexible. For example, it is impossible to have
every player on a defensive team practice each day against every
play the opponent runs. The skilled coach realizes this and selects
the most important plays in the opponent's repertoire. By limiting
the number of different plays he ensures that, within a reasonable
time span, each defensive player will get practice at stopping the
things the opponent does best. To plan to be on the field for longer
periods in pre-season practice may be necessary at times due to the
number of players on a roster or the magnitude of work to be done.

Planning long practices is always appealing because of the
potential to get a lot accomplished. There is, however, the fact that
after a period of time, players do lose their interest and ability to
concentrate. When this happens, time spent practicing is usually
wasted effort.

The worst type of long practices are those that are created by
the frustration of the coach. These usually occur when coaches become
angry over the lack of execution by their team. The old "we'll practice
it till we get it right" philosophy usually leads to frustration and
anger building. This creates a very negative teaching and learning
environment and can have a detrimental lasting effect on a team.

The logical progression involved in good coaching is to break down each technique or defensive scheme into segments or parts for teaching purposes; then start with the simplest, practice each part, and finally put the whole thing together. I have always felt that the organization of practice should reflect this type of progression, with individual drills occurring in the first part of practice and team work coming at the end.

THE PRACTICE PLAN

Pre-practice

It is important for each coach to get his players ready for practice. He does this mentally in meetings, and he must do it physically in the pre-practice period. In a five-minute time span, each coach puts his players through a warm-up routine. The primary purpose here is to get the players' bodies ready for practice. The routines that are used should incorporate skills and techniques that are basic and important to each position. This is not a drill-teaching period so the techniques used should be ones that are simple to execute and do not require the drills to be stopped for corrections. The objective here is to keep the players moving.

Examples of the types of movement drills that should be used are backpedaling, breaking on the ball, and catching drills for the defensive backs. The linebackers should warm up with movement drills that involve stretching, pass drops, break and drive on the thrown ball and catching drills. The defensive linemen should use movement drills that increase their flexibility, especially in the hip area. These drills usually involve various types of movements over dummies. Takeoff drills are excellent for the linemen, as are any types of activities that require changing directions.

Stretching

There is value in bringing the entire team together for an additional warm-up period where flexing or stretching exercises are employed. This period, which is eight to ten minutes in duration, is designed to stretch muscle groups that will be used in practice. The stretching exercises are most effective when they are directed by a trainer or conditioning or strength coach. Some teams use players to conduct this portion of the practice. I do not like using players since they are not used to direct any other part of practice. This is a very important activity with which to start practice and having a staff person lead it serves to emphasize its importance to team members.

Individual Practice and One-on-One

Individual Technique Periods

I do not think a football team should ever practice without a portion of it being devoted to individual technique work. In spring practice or pre-season work, longer portions of practice time will be devoted to this type of teaching and learning. During the regular season, the demands of specific team preparation dictate that more time be devoted to team drills than to individual work.

Further, it is not unreasonable to have as much as thirty minutes of a two-hour practice devoted to an individual technique period in a spring practice or early fall drills. With a long period it is not difficult to get a lot accomplished. It is, however, a real challenge to a coach when these periods are shortened due to the time demands of other drills. The really good coach is able to identify the few techniques that are critical to playing a position well and then to work on them during every practice regardless of the length of this period. Examples of crucial techniques for defensive positions would be using the hands to strike a blow for defensive linemen, pass drops for linebackers, and backpedaling for defensive backs. In addition, since tackling is the one skill every defensive player must be able to do well, it is not unreasonable to demand that every man work on some form of tackling drill every practice.

I have always felt that the best coaches are the ones who know how to teach technique. They identify a technique they want to coach and establish a way to teach it. The coach should break down each technique into steps or phases. Each part is taught separately until they are all practiced and the player understands what the coach wants in the way of executing the skill. After he has worked on all the parts, the player then executes the technique in its entirety. I like to refer to this type of teaching as the teaching alphabet. With the first or simplest phase of a technique representing the letter A, the next in order of difficulty B and so on, the coach teaches A, then goes to B, then teaches A again, then B and then goes on to C, back to A, B, C, D, back to A, until it is all learned.

I also think it is important to break down the teaching of individual techniques by the speed with which the player is asked to work. All technique teaching should start on a walk-through basis. This is a slow pace with very deliberate moves, enabling the player to feel each phase of a technique separately as he executes it. The next level is going through a technique at half speed. At this level, the player is still able to feel the phases of the technique as he executes, but it is done in a more fluid fashion. The final step is to actually do the technique at full speed. This is the velocity with which the player will be asked to perform in a game.

Many of the techniques involved with hitting or striking a blow can best be taught initially by using a sled or dummies to work against rather than another player. The advantage of using sleds or dummies is that the surface the defensive man is striking is in a predictable stationary position; also, because many sleds have multiple pads, many players can work at one time. After the basics of a technique have been acquired using a sled or dummies for an opponent, the next step is to practice the technique working against other defensive players who simulate offensive men. The next step is to work on the technique at full speed, one on one against offensive players.

One-on-One

The one-on-one periods are portions of the practice where defensive players work against offensive players. These are basically technique work periods but since they match offensive players against defensive players, the drills become competitive and intense. Although we all enjoy competitiveness in players, coaches must be careful not to get so caught up in the competitive aspect of these drills that they forget to coach the technique the drill was designed to develop. Examples of the most frequent and desirable one-on-one drills are the defensive line against the offensive line in one-on-one pass rush, the linebackers working against the running backs in one-on-one pass coverage, or the defensive backs covering the wide receivers and tight ends man-for-man. These drills can occur as part of individual work or can be done anywhere in the practice schedule. I prefer to do this one-on-one type of work early in practice.

Group Work

This period, much like the individual technique work, is much longer and consists more of a variety of drills in the pre-season or spring ball than it does during the regular season. Part of the reason this type of work is diminished during the regular season is lack of time to devote to it as well as the physical aspect of these drills.

Dive Drill

This drill involves all members of the football team, except the wide receivers and defensive backs. The offensive linemen and tight ends are the blockers, the defensive linemen and linebackers are the tacklers, the running backs carry the ball, and the quarterback is used to hand off. Boundaries within which the runner must carry the ball are marked off. It is a one-on-one blocking and defensive technique drill with the ball carrier given the opportunity to display his running skills in a confined area. The drill ends with the defensive man tackling the runner. This drill is highly competitive and there is a danger that players get so wrapped up in defeating each other that they forget to employ the techniques the drill is designed to evaluate.

Inside-run Drill

This drill is especially effective in teaching inside gap control in a defensive scheme. It involves the inside five defensive players, which comprises the three defensive linemen and the two inside linebackers in a thirty-four defense, or the four linemen and the middle linebacker in a four-three defense. The offensive personnel needed are the guards, tackles, center, quarterback, and at least one running back. The plays that are run by the offense are all inside plays and consist of dives, traps, isolation, and lead plays. The value of this drill is that it gives the defensive team an opportunity to get repetition on this part of the scheme, using only the people who are directly involved. The outside linebackers and secondary men can, while this drill is going on, be working on specifics that involve them. This is a very necessary drill, especially early in the implementation of a defensive scheme. It is a very physical drill and therefore cannot be implemented in a practice schedule every practice.

Perimeter Drill

While the interior five defensive players are working on the inside running game is a perfect time to schedule the perimeter drill in the practice plan. Since the perimeter drill requires offensive guards, running backs, and a quarterback, provisions must be made by the offensive coaches to rotate these players. This ensures that they all get inside as well as outside work, as the two drills are conducted simultaneously. The wide receivers and tight ends are the additional offensive players needed.

Defensively, the defensive backs and outside linebackers are involved. The offensive team runs all outside runs. A dummy is used to simulate a defensive end so that the tight end can block on it to show the blocking scheme as a key to the defensive backs. The perimeter run defenders have an excellent opportunity in this drill to work on all the different run force combinations. It is important that the offensive team vary the splits of the wide receivers and also run some plays to a tight weak side where there is no receiver split wide. This allows the corners as well as the safeties opportunities as primary force men.

Half-line Drill

This drill combines elements of the inside and perimeter drills. The defensive players involved are the nose tackle, defensive end, inside and outside linebacker, corner and safety on one side of the defensive team. The other inside linebacker is added to the drill if both guards are used by the offense. The remaining offensive personnel consists of a wide receiver, tight end, tackle, guard, center, quarterback, and two running backs. The offense runs running plays that are designed to attack the defense at every gap on a specific side. If perimeter runs are to be used that involve both guards pulling, then the offense needs to utilize two guards in their alignment. This drill is effective in teaching one of the scheme at a time, but the fact that there is a threat to only one side of the defense limits its value in the areas of keying and reacting.

Run Drill

Tight ends, outside linebackers, and a strong safety are added to the inside drill personnel to provide the players necessary to conduct a run drill. This is a high velocity drill in which the offense runs all its running plays inside and outside. However, the inside runs should outnumber the outside runs two to one. An occasional play-action pass called in the drill helps keep the defensive team honest in their reads. This drill pinpoints work on the total scheme as it applies to the running game. During the period the run drill is being conducted, the defensive backs can be going one on one in pass coverage against the defensive backs.

The inside, perimeter, half-line and run drills can all be used as full-speed tackling drills. I do not favor this, however, because the defense knows the limitation under which the offense is operating. By knowing this, the tacklers are really zeroed in on the running backs. All of this leads to too many high velocity big hits on the ball carriers in a confined area. In addition, when there is live tackling there is too much time spent unpiling after the tackle. These drills are very effective and are productive teaching aids without live tackling. All the offensive blocking and defensive techniques should be executed live and with high velocity to the point where the defenders are in a position to make a tackle on the ball carrier. At that point, the defender should tag the ball carrier or square up on him, break the ball carrier's momentum with his hands, and then pull away. Even though there is no live tackling, all players must run to be in a position to tag the ball carrier on every play. These drills should be conducted as scrimmages with no tackling.

Half-side Pass Skeleton

This drill is effective when it is desirable to isolate a specific side of the defense and work against it. For example, the right side defensive corner, safety, and outside and inside linebackers would work against pass patterns run by the left side of the offensive formation. A running back, tight end, and wide receiver, along with a quarterback, are the essential personnel offensively. This method of working on pass coverage is desirable in several specific situations. It is a good way to run pass skeleton if a team is short on personnel due to squad size, depth at a position, or injuries. It also allows the players on a specific side of the defense the opportunity to get a great many repetitions on specific strong- or weak-side pass patterns. In some situations, like when the zone defenses are being worked on, it is desirable to employ a free safety and the other inside linebackers in the drill. This is a problem in that a drill that was to involve work on a specific side is expanded to include players from the other side. When this happens the drill loses its effectiveness.

Under Pass Skeleton

The players who are most often used to defend the short zones in zone coverages or to cover the tight ends and running backs man-for-man in man coverages are the defensive players involved in this drill. They include the safeties and the inside and outside linebackers. Offensively, the tight end, running backs, and quarterback are involved. The offensive players run all short patterns and the defensive men execute their zone or man-for-man responsibilities.

The drill provides excellent opportunities for the short zone defenders to read patterns and drive on the thrown ball at proper angles. It also affords the defensive cover man occasion to work one-on-one, man-for-man coverage as well as a combination of in and out reads. The real value of the drill lies in the fact that these players can get a lot of repetitions on specifics while the other defensive players who are not directly involved are working in other areas.

Deep Pass Skeleton

This drill involves the four defensive backs and is designed to give them opportunities to make plays on deep throws. Very often, especially when a team uses mostly zone coverages, their defensive backs do not get the opportunity to defend deep passes because the ball is dropped off to short receivers so often. This drill forces the offense to throw deep routes due to its design. The offensive personnel involved are the wide receivers, tight ends, and the quarterback. The defense either rotates right or left into a three-deep zone or matches up man-for-man and plays either a free-safety man coverage or a blitz coverage with no free-safety help.

Pass Skeleton

Employing all the defensive players involved in pass coverage, the linebackers and the defensive backs, this drill affords excellent opportunities to work on all aspects of team pass coverage schemes. While this drill is being conducted is an excellent time for the defensive linemen to be working on pass rush against the offensive linemen. The offensive personnel involved are the wide receivers, tight ends, running backs, and quarterback. It is important that the offense vary its formations, pass patterns, and depths of drops by the quarterback so that the defensive men get maximum benefit from the drill. If the defensive players are forced to recognize formation variations, identify the various types of personnel in the game, and make adjustments, the drill is really beneficial. It is also important to work on specific down and distance situations in pass skeleton periods. This makes the practice more game-like and increases the value of pass skeleton in game preparation.

Pass Skeleton with Half-side Pass Rush

All the offensive and defensive personnel are involved in this drill. However, only one side of the offensive pass blockers and defensive pass rushers is used on each play. If the defense is using a three-man-line alignment, the outside linebacker, defensive end, inside linebacker, and nose tackle are designated as live pass rushers. The remaining defensive end takes a position on one knee and does not participate on that particular play. If a four-man-line defense is used, the tackle and end on a side are designated as live pass rushers along with the outside and middle linebackers. The offensive pass blockers are live on the side designated before the ball is snapped. The pass blockers on the opposite side relax on the play they are not involved in. All the pass defenders and pass receivers, including tight ends and running backs, are working on each play, just as they are in a regular pass skeleton. This drill is an excellent one to practice defending the pass along with working on pass rush. Most of the value that can be achieved in team pass drills is inherent in this drill without the potential for injury that is so probable when both sides of the defense are rushing at the same time. When team pass drills are run, injuries occur most frequently when players collide with each other in the area behind the offensive line of scrimmage. With team pass drills, too many players are placed in compromising positions in a congested area, thereby increasing the chances of injury.

Team Work

I think team work periods are most beneficial when they are separated into two categories. One is a run and play-action pass period and the other is a drop-back pass, draw, and screen period.

The value of adding the play-action passes to the run drill is that they are utilized by offensive teams in run situations. This, of course, means the threat of both the run and play action forces the defenders to play their keys and not overplay the run. The emphasis on the running game during this period should be on outside runs due to the fact that all the players involved in run force are in this drill.

The drop-back pass period utilizes all the elements involved in defending the pass. It is essential that the pass rushers rush hard on the initial phases of the rush but that as they approach the passer, they allow him to throw the ball in order that the coverage men get work at covering the receiver and playing the ball. It is also very important that draws and screens be incorporated along with drop-back passes. Since these are reaction-type plays and are used by the offense in drop-back pass situations, it is very important that they be a part of this particular practice period.

Specific Practice Game Situations

Pass Skeleton Inside the Plus 25-yard Line

As offensive teams move closer to their opponent's goal line, their passing philosophy is modified. Since there is less vertical area or depth to work with, the emphasis is on different types of routes and actions than they use farther out on the field. It is important that defensive teams have the opportunity to practice against pass offenses on this area of the field. It is an excellent idea to take a portion of the pass skeleton work each day inside the plus 25-yard line.

Pass Skeleton Two-Minute Situations

How a defensive team plays in the last two minutes of the first half or the last two minutes of a game very often determines whether or not it wins. The critical nature of these situations — when a team is ahead and the opponent's offense is trying to get in a scoring position — requires that practice time be allotted to them. This practice period must simulate the specific situations with the game clock, score in the game, and timeouts remaining as factors as the drill is being conducted. Pass skeleton is a good way to practice these situations, but ultimately the whole defensive team has to work in these areas. This is due to the fact that every defensive player must know how he has to react in the specific situations when the opponent is trying to conserve time.

Team Short-yardage and Goal-line Situations

Offensive teams usually change their philosophy in terms of use of formations, players in the game, as well as plays used when they are in short-yardage and goal-line situations. It is important then that defensive teams devote a portion of their team practice periods each week to these areas. Since the amount of time a team can set aside to work on these specific offenses is limited, a defensive team needs to have as much carryover as possible from their regular defenses in these situations. Although specific modifications in the way of coverages and alignments may be necessary, the defensive teams that usually perform the best against short-yardage and goal-line offenses are those that need to make only minor adjustments in their basic schemes.

10

Scouting
The
Opponent

Football coaching has been affected by the high-tech age right along with every other form of human endeavor. Computers have reduced the amount of time needed to compile information, printouts have replaced handwritten scouting reports, and videotape has replaced movie film. Some even say the game itself has changed because of all the discoveries modern technology has contributed to football.

It is hard to argue with the fact that there are some differences in football today as compared to the game in the not-too-distant past. The players are bigger, stronger, and faster due to the advances made in the areas of training, conditioning, and nutrition. The game is played on a faster field manufactured by man, in some cases indoors, under near-perfect conditions. All these things would lead one to believe modern football is a different game than it was twenty-five years ago.

Although some aspects have changed through the years, the game itself is the same. It still has as its foundation blocking, tackling, running, passing, and catching. It continues to be a game set aside from most others by the physical contact aspect. It is still a game that requires great commitment on the part of the individual player to play it well.

In the area of coaching, the use of videotape has enabled coaches to critique practices and games while they are in progress, rather than having to wait three or four hours after the event to see the movie film. Without question, this has afforded coaches the opportunity to be more effective teachers. However, the computer has been the device that has enabled coaches to progress more than any other. By utilizing the computer in opponent scouting, coaches save hundreds of hours and amass much more information than they did in the days before computers were used in football.

I have always felt that anyone can accumulate information on an opponent's offense. I do not believe there is any unique skill associated with this activity. The skill comes in utilizing the information. Questions must be answered, such as, how much of the information is useful to both players and coaches? What part of it is applicable only to the coaches in game planning and what is essential information to get to the players? I think skillful coaches make these judgments and get full use of the materials available. Many inexperienced coaches are guilty of trying to give their players too much information. In their zeal to be thorough, they give them so much to learn that they learn nothing well. Again, I think if a coach selects those pieces of information that apply to each individual player, and emphasizes them all week long in preparation, the player will be better prepared than if he is confused by volumes of material he can't assimilate.

There are some dangers in using the computer to the point of removing the human element. There is always a certain amount of paperwork involved in scouting reports and game plans that I feel coaches should do manually. I know that if someone writes something down several times, he learns it and becomes somewhat expert on that material. If, however, he lets the computer compose all the reports, he does not have the benefit of the learning experience. I feel strongly that there are some dangers if the game becomes too high tech. Although progress is necessary, I do not think coaches can let the game get too far away from its dependence on people for its identity.

THE CRITICAL FACTORS

Personnel

The makeup of the offensive team from a personnel standpoint is the first consideration in scouting an opponent. It is important to determine the strengths and weaknesses of a team's offensive personnel in order to develop a plan to stop them. The size, speed, and skill matchups are the critical factors here. It is also important to evaluate how the opponent uses its personnel in specific situations. An example of this would be when a third wide receiver is put in the game, is he more likely to be a decoy or a primary receiver? If a team uses a formation with two tight ends, are they more inclined to run to the side of one than the other? Or, is one of the tight ends used more as a pass receiver than the other?

Players always like to know how big, fast, and tough their opponents are. The coaches should present this information to them. However, they should also encourage them to study their opponent carefully as they watch films or tapes all week long. Of course, if these types of visual aids are not available, the coach must provide all the information.

It is the job of each position coach to teach his players what to look for in film- or tape-viewing sessions. Many times players will look at film as a fan does for entertainment and waste time that could be used for learning. For example, the defensive linemen should be taught to study their opponent and look for any tips that the offensive linemen may be giving by their alignment, including their splits, by whether they are deeper or closer to the line, or by the amount of weight or pressure they put on the hands they have down in their stances. If a lineman takes a big split on a running down, it could mean there is less chance of a wide run on his side because most offensive teams tighten their splits to shorten the corner when they run wide. If he lines up close to the line of scrimmage on a run down, there is a better chance he will fire out and base block than pull, which usually occurs when an offensive lineman lines up deeper. The general rule is that the offensive lineman will have more weight forward or on his hand in his stance when he is run blocking and will have more weight back or less pressure on his hand when he is pass blocking. These same types of specific things to look for or tendencies exist for each defensive player. It is the coach's responsibility to educate the players as to what they should look for as they study their opponent.

Formations

The formation tendencies or what types of running and passing plays the opponent runs from each of their alignments is really the basis for the defensive game plan. The opponent's formations determine the type of adjustments that have to be made in a team's defensive scheme. Every offensive formation has strengths and weaknesses. Some create better chances for offensive success running, while others are most suited to passing.

There are some general rules or tendencies that are inherent in offensive formations. Generally, the tighter formations are, the better suited they are for running. They put more blockers in a position to block the defensive players. In contrast, the more wide-open or the more the offensive players are distributed over the width of the field, the more the formation is suited for passing. Obviously the tighter running formations have the effect of compressing or squeezing the area the defense must defend, while the more wide open formations force each defender to play defense in a much larger area. It is very important for the defense to determine how the opponent is using variations in their offensive formations to put pressure on the defense.

Running Game

The first consideration is the opponent's running game. A defensive team must establish its physical dominance by shutting down the run. It is therefore paramount that the opponent's best running plays be identified from each formation and adjustments be made in the defensive scheme to stop them. This includes any slants or line charge variations that put defensive linemen or linebackers in a better position to make plays against the inside running game. These changeups are used as specific adjustments against specific formations and are designed to take away the team's most productive inside runs.

Most offensive teams run the ball more effectively to the tight-end side of the formation than they do to the open side or the side away from the tight end. There are not a lot of good running plays away from the tight-end side. The two formation variations that offensive teams use most frequently to run the ball outside are to vary the splits of the receivers and to change personnel by substituting a tight end for a wide receiver. By tightening the split of the wide receiver by alignment or motion, he is placed in a better position to block a defender to his inside. Substituting a second tight end for a wide receiver gives the offense a much bigger player better equipped to block than a wide receiver. The additional tight end in the game can be used to block in tandem on the strong side or as a tight-end blocker on the weak side.

The plan to defend the outside or perimeter runs must include adjustments in the run forces to best defend against these formation variations.

Play-action Passes

Play-action passes are passing plays that are designed to be thrown after the quarterback fakes a running play. Obviously these plays are most effective when they are run from the same formation in the same situations as the companion running play. These play-action fakes are designed to hold the short defenders, primarily the linebackers, and keep them from getting depth in their pass drops.

After the play-action passes that a team runs from the various formations are identified, it is important that adjustments in the pass coverage schemes be made to put defenders in a position to make plays. Many times a particular coverage is effective in forcing the runs of a particular formation but the normal pattern reads place players in bad positions to make plays against the play-action passes. This is when adjustments have to be made, especially in the zone coverages, in the way the defenders read patterns. When zone coverages are employed, special attention must be paid to specific pattern-read adjustments when both backs release either to the strong or weak side of the formation. This flow action creates a numbers advantage for the offense and must be compensated for by the defense adjusting the pattern read to get additional defenders in coverages to the overload side of the formation. Bootlegs or other types of counter action passes also require that specific adjustments be made in the way the patterns are read and in the coverage men deployed in zone coverages.

Drop-back Passes

The ideal way to stop an opponent's pass offense is to always be in a situation in zone coverages where the pass defenders outnumber the receivers to the side where the passer is throwing the ball. If a man-for-man defense is called, the best guarantee of a successful defensive play is to have the best coverage men matched up with the opponent's best receivers with no mismatches. By determining an offensive team's pass tendencies in formations, defensive teams are able to set their pass coverages to win the numbers game in the zones and ensure favorable matchups in man-for-man coverage. If, for example, an offensive team uses an alignment as a weak-side passing formation a high percentage of the time, the defense must make the necessary adjustments in their pass coverage.

Two things are absolutely essential in the way of coverage adjustments. One is that whenever the opponent uses this formation and a zone defense is called, a weak-zone defense should be the automatic defense played. If a strong zone is played, the pattern read for the hook defender on the strong side, with a weak pass action, should be such as to cause him to work to cover on the weak side. If a man-for-man defense is to be played, the men who are covering on the weak side should have the skill to cover the receivers on that side. If they do not match up well, adjustments must be made by moving personnel around to get the best coverage men on their best receivers. The other option is to give double coverage help to the defenders who are at the biggest coverage disadvantage.

Another critical factor in scouting the opponent's formation passing tendencies is to determine how the offensive team is using its running backs as receivers. What type of flare controls do they use? Are their backs always checking to see if linebackers are blitzing before they release or are there times when one back or the other is free releasing with no blocking assignment while the other back blocks. Some formations are better suited to get one back or the other into the pass pattern. When the defense identifies the passing tendencies or flare controls from each offensive formation, the game plan must contain coverage adjustments to take advantage of this information.

The types of pass protections a team uses are very often predictable by formation. This knowledge is essential in game planning. By knowing the protection a team uses from each alignment, the defensive team can use the best possible combination of linebackers and linemen as rushers to pressure the passer.

Down and Distance

Which defensive fronts and coverages a team will use in each down-and-distance situation is determined by the down-and-distance tendencies of the offensive team. Before a defensive game plan can be devised, the formation and specific plays used by the offense in first and ten, second and short (six or less yards to go), second and long (seven or more yards to go), third and long (three or more yards to go) and third and short (two or less yards to go) must be compiled. These tendencies or frequencies with which the offense does things determine the defenses and coverages that will be used in the specific down-and-distance situations.

In addition to compiling the plays the offensive team uses, it is also important to determine how the offense uses personnel in these situations. For example, if an offensive team uses a formation with three wide receivers on second and long, the defensive calls would be different than they would be if a three-tight-end formation were used. In these types of situations, the defensive plan must include the option of substituting to match the offensive personnel on the field. The two down-and-distance situations where the offense substitutes personnel the most are third down and short and third down and long. In short yardage the wide receivers are usually replaced by tight-end blockers and in long yardage the tight end is replaced with a third wide receiver.

SPECIAL SITUATIONS

Short Yardage

It is important for a defensive team to know how the offense approaches third or fourth down and short. For example, many teams treat third or fourth down and one yard to go as a true short-yardage down, send multiple tight ends in the game for wide receivers, and try to power run the ball. If a team uses this approach, the only passes they would throw in this situation are play-action passes used as an element of surprise. If a team keeps its regular offensive people on the field in short-yardage situations with two yards to go, they are keeping available the options of a balanced attack. By not substituting, they are in a better position to have a more diversified passing attack yet retain the option of running the ball.

Each of these specific situations requires different types of responses from the defensive teams. The defensive game plan must contain fronts, coverage changeups, and a substitution plan to defend against the variety of approaches an offensive team may take in short yardage.

The particular defenses a team chooses to use in short yardage are implemented because they have the best chance of stopping the opponent's offense. Short-yardage defenses do not have to be different from the team's base defensive scheme. In fact, if a team has a good defensive scheme, what they play in short yardage should be simply their base defense with short-yardage adjustments.

Goal Line

Most offensive teams substitute tight ends for wide receivers when they get the ball inside their opponent's 5-yard line. Which players they put in the game and the specific types of formations they use are important factors. The use of the tighter formation increases chances of running the ball, especially with the power-run game, but decreases the chances of a balanced passing attack. Some other critical factors in scouting the goal-line offense of the opponent: What yard line does the ball have to be on for them to send their substitutes into the game? How do they feature their personnel in these situations? Do they have a favorite back they give the ball to when they must get it? On what yard line or in what situation do they return normal personnel to the field to open up the offense? These are all critical questions that must be answered within the information accumulated in the scouting process.

Goal-line defenses do not very often resemble the alignments used by a team in other situations. The need for more big men on the field to counter the personnel the offense is using at times requires a radical deviation from the normal scheme. This is seen especially in teams whose defensive base scheme involves three-down linemen but who to a four-man-line goal-line defense. Even though, in this situation, the alignment is substantially different, there must be as much carryover in techniques and adjustments as possible.

Inside the Plus 25-yard Line

Offensive teams are forced to make modifications in their passing offense as they move the ball closer to their opponent's goal line. The pass offenses change because there is less area to work within running patterns vertically or from a depth standpoint. The design of the passing game also changes due to the fact that man coverage can be anticipated a much higher percentage of the time at this point than it can be out on the field. Most of the routes are designed to take advantage of man-for-man coverage variations. It is very important to be able to pinpoint the types of modifications the team makes in their passing game inside the plus 25-yard line and devise a plan to stop them. The ability of a defensive team to keep an opponent from scoring when they have possession in this area is one of the big momentum-changing events that can occur in a game. Again, it is really important that a defensive team be able to play their base scheme in these situations with minor adjustments and not have to devise something entirely new. For example, a team that plays mostly zone does not have to change and play man-for-man coverage just because the opponent has the ball inside the plus 25-yard line. In fact, zone coverages can be very effective, with minor adjustments in the drops and pattern reads, in shutting down the pass offenses that are designed to beat man coverages.

DEVELOPING THE GAME PLAN

I really believe in carrying the "team" concept of working together into the coaching area as well. A defensive staff should work as a group as much as possible, especially when they are in the process of evaluating an opponent and establishing a game plan. It is much more effective for a staff to study film or tapes of the opponent together. This approach gives each coach the opportunity to express his interpretation of what he sees and encourages reaction from other members of the group.

A certain amount of independent work is necessary in accumulating information but the more a staff can work together, the less chance there is for misinterpretation, misunderstanding, and as a result, inefficiency.

After the coaching staff has accumulated the information on the opponent through the scouting process, the next step is to use it to devise a game plan. This plan should represent the thinking of the head coach and the entire defensive staff. Each member should have the opportunity to express his views in each area. The defensive coordinator has the responsibility to make final decisions on all aspects and to determine how best to implement the plan.

The defensive coordinator has another very important responsibility in game planning and that is not to let the defensive staff get so caught up in what the opponent does that they lose sight of the important issue of focus as it relates to the defensive team. If the coaches are able to keep in mind the basic objective to outexecute the opponent's offense, then the game plan will merely reflect the defensive base scheme being adjusted to the opponent's offense. If, however, the defensive staff is so concerned about the opponent's offense that they lose sight of the adaptability of their system, the urge will be to devise new and different schemes to stop the opponent's offense. This type of overreaction to the opponent most often leads to a defensive team's beating itself through its own errors and overall inefficiency.

The best game plans are those that involve little, if any, new learning. There should be great similarity from week to week in both the form and substance of the plan. If the players are not asked to learn a lot of new things each week, they can focus on doing those things that will make them better players. There is a cumulative effect in that players who have the opportunity to execute the same techniques over and over inevitably get better. There is also a need to have a commitment to technique if a team is going to rely on outexecuting the opponent. Teams that do a lot of new things defensively each week do not have the practice time to do much technique work. They must spend their practice time learning new schemes designed to confuse their opponent. These teams rely on fooling the opponent's offense, not on outexecuting them.

The game plan itself must start with making the adjustments in the base scheme that will take away the best runs of the opponent. The defensive team must be prepared to take away the things the offense does best. This is accomplished by adjusting the shades or alignments of the defensive linemen and linebackers. The idea is to make slight changes in the defense to place more players at the point of attack than the offense can block. The plan should also include a way for the defense to move or slant the defensive linemen into gaps aggressively on the snap of the ball. The objective here is to get more defensive men at the point of attack than the offense can block, as well as to create more difficult blocking angles. These types of movements involve merely changing gap responsibilities by movement on the snap of the ball. They can involve the entire defensive line slanting in one direction or they can involve only a defensive end or tackle taking a gap aggressively on the snap of the ball. As is the case with changing the shades, line change variations must be designed to take away specific parts of the opponent's running offense. Again, they are only variations or adjustments in the defensive team's base scheme.

The other aspect of the run defense plan is the run force. Again, any adjustments that are made in the area should be the ones the perimeter defenders are accustomed to making. For example, if a team is primarily a safety run force team but goes to corner force when the wide receiver is in a tight split, they should continue to make the same adjustments each week. This ensures continuity and reduces the chances for mental errors, which can result in a big play by the offense. Run forces are built into coverages. The type of pass coverage used dictates the force that is to be used on each play. On running downs, the primary consideration in the game plan must be to place the perimeter defender people in the best possible position to force the run. The run force in zone defenses is much more effective than it is in man-to-man coverages. As a result, there is no doubt that the game plan should be made up primarily of defenses that utilize zone coverages in run-down situations.

It is always good to have one good run-down blitz as part of the game plan. Again, however, this blitz should be one the team knows, has practiced, and is adjustable to all types of formations and plays. New blitzes each week only cause a team to compromise their margin by increasing the opportunity for the opponent to make a big play.

The game plan to stop the opponent's pass game should reflect adjustments in coverages, not new designs and concepts. Adjustments in the pattern reads in the zones and the creation of favorable matchups in the man coverages is really the basis for the game plan to stop the pass. If the matchups cannot be worked out to be favorable for the defense, the plan must compensate with double coverage to eliminate unfavorable situations. Whenever these kinds of problems become too frequent or difficult to solve, the emphasis should go to more zone and less man-for-man coverage in the game plan.

In the base defenses of most teams, effective pass rush comes from a defensive rusher beating an offensive blocker. Whenever the defense is put in a position of not being able to rush effectively because of poor physical matches, variations in the scheme must be employed. Games and stunts designed to vary the rush lanes are effective changeups in rushing the passer. They must be selected on the basis of their potential effectiveness in creating more desirable one-on-one situations or taking advantage of pass protection schemes. Games and stunts must be used as occasional changeups to the base or straight rush. Part of their value lies in the surprise element and of course if they are overused, this particular advantage becomes nonexistent. Another effective way to pressure the passer is to vary the number of rushers used on a specific down. Alternating rushers is another way to add variety to the pass rush. Varying the type of pass rush used has the effect of reducing the predictability factor for the offense which affects the timing of the passing game.

Even though a defensive team does not blitz frequently in passing situations, their game plan should include at least one blitz designed to pressure the passer. The particular blitz a team selects to use from its base package should be the one that will cause the biggest protection problems for the offense as well as leave the defense with the best possible coverage matchups. Again, it is not important that a team blitz frequently. The critical factor is that the opponent must always feel there is the threat of the blitz. If this threat doesn't exist, the opponent's passer is able to function with the confidence that he will have the time to throw any pattern at any time he chooses.

The extent to which nickel defenses are a part of the game plan depends on whether or not the offensive team uses formations with three or four receivers on passing downs. If they do substitute this personnel, it is necessary for the defense to respond with their substitute defenses. Since these are passing situations, the type of coverages to be used must be established first. These coverages must be part of the defensive team's base nickel coverage scheme. Basically, two types of general plans have to be developed. One is the coverages to be used in shorter yardage situations when the offense has three to six yards to go to make a first down. The coverages to be used in these relatively short down and distances will be mostly man-for-man or blitz coverages. These coverages are designed to challenge receivers and take away the short passing games. The specific coverages used will depend on who the favorite receivers are and how they are used in these situations.

The other plan that has to be developed is to determine the type of nickel coverages to be used when the offense has more than six yards to go to convert a third down into a first down. In these types of situations, the plan should consist of a variety of coverages including zone, man for man and blitz. The addition of zone to the nickel coverages in the long yardage situation has the effect of making the quarterback's reads more complex, thereby reducing his efficiency.

The pass rushes used in conjunction with the nickel coverages should be developed with the goal of creating the best possible matchups to pressure the passer. If an offensive team runs the football in these nickel situations, the defensive players must be alerted to this fact. However, no attempt should be made to specifically defense the run with the pass rushers. If the latter is done, its effect is to slow down the rush and make it less effective because the rushers are clearing any threats of run before they can rush. The game plan in nickel situations should always be to rush the passer, play pass coverage, and react to the run should one occur.

The game plan to cover the special situations that occur in a game like short yardage, goal line, inside the plus 25-yard line and two minutes, should, as much as possible, consist of adjustments in or modifications of a team's base defense. Each of these special situations can come at critical points in a game and effective execution, or the lack of it, can mean the difference between winning and losing. The defensive players should, therefore, be executing techniques and schemes they know and have confidence in. This gives them their best chance to be successful.

There is a real temptation to create special defenses for all of these situations. However, not enough practice time can be devoted to these specific areas to learn new schemes well. There must be as much carryover as possible from the team's base defense.

The plan must also include a defense to be played if the offensive team lines up in an unusual formation that none of the normal defensive adjustments fit. This is usually some type of maximum coverage alignment utilizing zone coverage designed to prevent a big play by the offense.